Studying English Literature

This practical guide provides students beginning to study literature at university with the reading and writing skills needed to make the most of their degree. It begins by explaining the history of the subject and of literary criticism in an easily digestible form. The book answers the key questions every first-year English student wants to ask: how to approach assignments and reading lists, how to select the best online resources, how to make effective notes to retain and use what you've read, how to write an essay, how to find something to say when you're stuck, and how to construct your argument. It contains key tips on grammar, style and references, and examples of real student essays, with explanations of what works and what doesn't. Both for those beginning English degrees and for those considering studying English, this book will be an essential purchase.

Tory Young is Senior Lecturer in English at Anglia Ruskin University, Cambridge.

Studying English Literature
A Practical Guide

TORY YOUNG

CAMBRIDGE
UNIVERSITY PRESS

CAMBRIDGE UNIVERSITY PRESS
Cambridge, New York, Melbourne, Madrid, Cape Town, Singapore, São Paulo,
Delhi, Dubai, Tokyo

Cambridge University Press
The Edinburgh Building, Cambridge CB2 8RU, UK

Published in the United States of America by Cambridge University Press, New York

www.cambridge.org
Information on this title: www.cambridge.org/9780521690140

First published 2008
Fourth printing 2010

Printed in United Kingdom at the University Press, Cambridge

A catalogue record for this publication is available from the British Library

ISBN 978-0-521-86981-2 hardback
ISBN 978-0-521-69014-0 paperback

For Mark

Contents

Chapter 4 Essays

Chapter 5 Sentences

Chapter 6 References

Acknowledgements

Since I began to teach academic writing, I have been privileged to meet and learn from some of the most inspiring innovators in the field. I am particularly grateful to the following: Rebecca Stott and Simon Avery for allowing me to work with them on Anglia Ruskin University's *Speak–Write* Project; Catherine Maxwell for introducing me to *Thinking Writing* at Queen Mary, University of London, and Sally Mitchell and Alan Evison themselves for allowing me to participate in the events of this programme; all the staff of the John S. Knight Institute for Writing in the Disciplines, but in particular Jonathan Monroe and Katy Gottschalk, whose influence during the two summers I spent at the Cornell Consortium for Writing in the Disciplines provoked a decisive change in my thinking; Lisa Ganobcsik-Williams for her thorough knowledge of the ways that writing is taught on both sides of the Atlantic and her generosity in sharing it with me: both she and David Morley have offered intellectual and practical support for my work and this project. As a lecturer in English Literature, I'm happy to have worked among dedicated colleagues at Anglia Ruskin University – Katy Price, Catherine Silverstone, Alison Ainley, Rick Allen, Nora Crook and Mary Joannou have been especially supportive – and to teach highly engaged and engaging students such as Tracey Tingey and Alex Hobbs, who have kindly allowed me to reproduce their essays. My friends and colleagues at the London Modernism Seminar Anna Snaith and Maggie Humm helpfully provided information about writing and grading practices in their respective universities. In New York, Mark Macbeth was a superlative host and guide to the CCCC and the city when the conference was held there. A particularly big thank you is due to Rebecca Beasley and Markman Ellis who put me up in style when I was working in the British Library. I am thankful to the readers of the initial proposal and final manuscript of *Studying English Literature*, whose suggestions were invaluable, to Margaret Berrill, the copy-editor, for important suggestions and corrections, and to Cambridge University Press for their continued patience in the gestation of the project. Since I started working on it, I am thrilled to have become daughter-in-law of Jo Anderson and Bill Currie, whose conversations about literature and language I relish. As ever, I thank Robert, Jane and Edward Young, and Miriam Lynn for their love and support, but the beginning, middle and end of the story lies with Mark Currie, to whom I dedicate this book.

Chapter 1

Introduction

1.1 What this book is about

This is a book for literature students. It seeks to answer some basic questions about the role of literature in society, the nature of literature as an academic subject, and the relationship between reading within and outside the university. It intends to provoke you into reconsidering the role of literature in your life, the ways in which you have read stories, and the ways in which they have shaped you. Above all, through an examination of these issues, it seeks to improve your writing and your reading. The process begins with a series of reflections on the reciprocity of the relationship between writing and reading, and with some ideas about the value, in history and now, of reading and writing to powerful social institutions such as education, government and the media.

Why have you chosen to study literature? There are of course many possible answers to this question, but it seems likely that any answer would refer in some way to reading or writing. I would hazard a guess that it is your passion for reading, rather than a confidence in your ability as a critical writer, that has determined your choice. Do you consider yourself to be good at writing? What would it mean to be a good reader? And why do we frequently question our abilities as writers, but not as readers?

I ask these questions to draw attention to a significant premise of *Studying English Literature*. Critical writing does not exist independently in isolation from other facets of literature and literary study such as reading, oral argument, silent thought processes or creative writing. The main aim of this book is to improve your reading, writing and thinking about literature. Inevitably this will involve some study of what have been termed the technicalities or mechanics of writing: grammar, register, generic conventions and disciplinary guidelines (see especially chapters 5: Sentences and 6: References). However, to focus entirely upon these mechanical aspects would be not only dull and prescriptive, but it might also suggest a narrow formula for good writing, or that there is only one way to construct an essay, or that this formula is disconnected from what you actually want to say. This book stresses the importance of actually *having* something to say – it returns argument and substance back to the heart of effective writing. General guides to essay writing that focus primarily on structure can obscure the real obstacles to effective writing and can fail to recognise the contexts that shape and determine your writing, the way that you think about writing, and the things that you are writing about. This book is concerned with the writing that you are going to undertake while studying literature at university, but it will not forget that this takes place in the wider context of who you are in the world. We will examine the nature of writing in the academic context and the particular subject in the following chapters but, to begin with, I want to invite you to consider your own reading and writing, and to try and uncover your own ingrained beliefs and anxieties. We can begin to understand our relationship to academic writing through becoming conscious of the role writing has played in our lives to date, and of our learning experiences.

1.2 Some practicalities: how to use this book

First, there are some practical things and some terminology that you need to know to fully engage with this book and to prepare for your experience at university.

1.2.1 Some practicalities: the logbook

Throughout this book, you'll find boxes that invite you to note your responses to the issues I have raised. I urge you to keep a laptop, or notebook and pen, with you as you read. The notes that you make as you respond will prove invaluable in helping you to absorb new information and challenging ideas; they will also form an aide-mémoire for helpful reflection on what you have learnt, and how your ideas might have changed as you progress through your studies. Many institutions will ask you to reflect upon your learning during your degree – this might even form part of a final assignment, so you might be able to use these notes as preparation for a later task. Even if you are not assessed on your learning experience as a whole in this way, you might be asked to keep logbooks in which you record reflections upon and impressions of individual courses. These logbooks are like diaries; you write in them regularly, informally – perhaps in note form – and date each entry. But even if this is not a course requirement, I strongly recommend the practice: getting into the habit of writing as a daily activity will prevent writer's block, it will help break down the fear that an essay question and a blank sheet of paper can instil. The logbook is usually a private text, although the notes you make in it may form the basis of a later more formal and public document. Paradoxically, although the logbook writing is informal, the regular practice of writing in it will enable you to take yourself seriously as a writer, which is one of the chief objectives of this book. Stressing the importance of the logbook also gives me an early opportunity to raise some of the key principles of how you can really improve your reading and writing, as they have also been outlined by the *Thinking Writing* project at Queen Mary, University of London (www.thinkingwriting.qmul.ac.uk).

Some key principles
- Informal writing is important; it concentrates the mind
- Reading and writing go together
- Reading and writing develop through practice and reflection

1.2.2 Some practicalities: terminology relating to university

This book is intended for readers who are either students at the start of degree-level literary study or for people who are preparing for it. In chapter 2: Reading, I consider in more detail the complexities of some terms that are used widely in literary study, such as **text**, but here I'll define some words that relate to the institutions of higher education. This gives me a chance to introduce another key principle: when you are reading you should always look up words that you don't know or are unsure about in their particular context, and make a note of their meanings. You cannot fully engage with literary or critical texts unless you understand their lexis; in seeking to do so you will also improve your own vocabulary and thus write with more style and specificity.

Another key principle
- Always read with a dictionary to hand

Throughout this book I will refer to the **subject** or **discipline** of literature, or literature as a **field of study** and use these terms somewhat synonymously to refer to the teaching of literature. Discipline is a word with interesting resonances, however, that are worth reflecting on for a moment. I am using it here to denote 'a department of learning or knowledge' (*OED*) but it has two other connotations; firstly 'of disciples' and secondly 'of punishment, correction and training'. How do you think these three are related? They can be linked to an idea of education that is becoming outmoded in some places (but

Dictionaries and critical guides

When studying literary texts, a good dictionary such as the *Oxford English Dictionary* should suffice (http://dictionary.oed.com; if you are in the UK you can even use your mobile phone to obtain the *OED*'s definitions, see www.askoxford.com), but when you are reading a work of criticism, a glossary of critical terms, such as Lentricchia and McLaughlin's *Critical Terms for Literary Study* (1995), will provide the precise definitions as they are utilised in the academic discipline of literature. The Penguin dictionaries of *Literary Terms and Literary Theory* and *Critical Theory* are up-to-date, comprehensive and lucid; a longer and more provocative overview to selected key terms in contemporary literary study is provided by Andrew Bennett and Nicholas Royle's *Introduction to Literature, Criticism and Theory*. Ian Littlewood's *Literature Student's Survival Kit* is an invaluable encyclopedia of information about the Bible, Classical mythology, maps, movements and historical timelines.

is firmly upheld in others): that education is the transfer of knowledge from one master to a group of obedient believers and the idea of disciples elevates the status of the knowledge that is being transferred to that of a religious truth; that it has a strict regime of rules and regulations to be followed if chastisement is to be avoided. When we look briefly, as we will below, at the histories of literacy, schooling and the subject of literature, we can see that these formulations have been integral to their development, and in particular the crucial role that the Christian Church has played in the West.

Another term that displays the historical origins of a familiar idea is **academia**, which now means all universities, colleges and the work that takes place within them but originally referred to Plato's Academy, the school of philosophers who comprised it. As we shall see in chapter 3: Argument, these fourth-century BC philosophers had a reputation for scepticism, questioning all knowledge and belief systems, things that are deemed 'natural' or 'common sense', their truth status usually unchallenged. One of the intentions of this book is to encourage you to recognise and take up your position as a critical writer within the modern-day **academy**, perhaps to challenge things that are normally taken for granted.

Other terminology is perhaps less provocative but may be unfamiliar due to local and national variances. In the US (and countries that follow an American higher education system), in the first year of study you will be known as a **freshman**, regardless of your gender, while in the UK, you might be known as a **fresher** (although this label is used more specifically to refer to the very early stages of your study, perhaps just the first few weeks). All students who are in the process of studying for a degree are known as **undergraduates** while people who go on to further study (such as MAs, which are taught courses in humanities subjects, and PhDs, which are longer independent research projects) are known collectively as **graduates**, as are all the ex-students who have completed and passed their degrees (hence such phrases as 'graduate careers'). Beware that there are some variations in the use of MA: at Oxford and Cambridge, this award can be conferred three or four years after graduating without the student having undertaken any further study; in Scotland, it is sometimes used to refer to an undergraduate degree. In Scotland, the undergraduate Honours degree lasts four, not three years, although an Ordinary degree can be awarded after three years' study. In the US, **school** can refer to college or university, while in the UK, school is the place of education until you are sixteen or eighteen. The way that academics, the people who teach and supervise you, are referred to also depends upon which side of the Atlantic you are on (or aligned to); in the US the word **professor** (with a small 'p') means a tutor who has usually completed a PhD and has a record of publication, while in the UK this person is known as a **lecturer**; their names are prefaced by the title 'Dr', indicating that their PhDs have passed examination by academic specialists. An **associate or assistant professor**, another US term, is simply someone who has secured employment but who may not yet have been granted a permanent job. Confusingly, meanwhile, someone addressed as **Professor** (with a capital 'p' when used as a title in place of Dr or Ms) is at the pinnacle of the academic profession, and has been awarded a **chair** (a job with a title, for example, the Chair of Contemporary Writing) in recognition of the contribution she or he has made to her or his field of study; this is the only use of the word 'professor' in the UK. To avoid confusion, in this book when I refer to the lecturers, teaching assistants or professors who teach you, I will use the word **tutors** to comprise them all. Although the term **academics** could also be used, it encompasses a larger set of people including researchers, who may not be involved in teaching undergraduates; a slightly old-fashioned, although still current, synonym for academics is **scholars**.

Each academic year is divided into either two **semesters** or three shorter **terms** in which teaching takes place. In modular systems, there is usually assessment (graded essays or exams) during and at the end of each term or semester, followed by vacations in which you are expected to pursue your own reading and study. During term-time, it is likely that your contact with tutors will be composed of some or all of the following activities: lectures, seminars, tutorials, individual supervisions and, increasingly, web-based communications. In **lectures** one member of staff talks about a specified topic for approximately one hour, sometimes with the aid of audio-visual equipment and handouts. **Seminars** are more informal groups (varying from about eight to thirty depending on the institution) where you are encouraged to discuss and question course texts and topics in the presence of a tutor, although conversation might be led by a fellow student. Seminars ordinarily last between one and three hours. **Tutorials** are much smaller meetings of a tutor with one or up to seven students who have had more freedom in selecting the texts under consideration. **Individual supervisions** occur when you need to see a tutor about a specific topic, perhaps for a dissertation or graded essay; such sessions are not normally timetabled but happen when you make an appointment or visit staff members during their office hours. Increasingly, you will find that the Internet is used as a resource where lecture notes, discussion topics, questions, comments and extracts relating to your course, as well as informal exchanges, are posted on **Blackboard** or **WebCT**.

Depending upon your particular institution your units of study may be called **courses**, **modules** or **units**; they may have straightforwardly descriptive names, *The Nineteenth-Century Novel*, for example, or more alluring ones, like *Victorian Worlds and Underworlds*. Some will be optional and some compulsory. In general, the kinds of courses that you will study at first will be broad introductions and overviews; as you progress you are likely to be offered more specialised and diverse options. The final award that you will receive at the end of your degree (First Class Honours, for example) again will vary according to your locality but it is likely to be determined by marks that you have gained after the first year of full-time study. Usually, it is only necessary to pass the first year but these marks won't count towards your final degree. Your university will publish the criteria for the different grades (First, Upper Second, Lower Second, Third, Fail in the UK or A, B, C, D and F in the US) in your departmental handbook or on its website (see chapter 4: Essays for some examples).

1.3 Reading and writing in your life

It is a popular assumption that literature students are good at writing because they have an interest in (other people's) writing. But perhaps this statement makes you feel slightly anxious: you – or your teachers – may well have questioned your ability to write in a way that you have not questioned your ability to read. What is the defining quality of literature students then? Is it that they are good at reading books? Or that they are good at writing about books? I have said that this book is about the reciprocity of reading and writing. This chapter will consider the boundaries between reading and writing, how they were erected, and how we might dismantle them. In doing so it will consider the social value of literacy, explain something of its history and contemplate its future. It will consider the explorations of reading and writing, creativity and criticism that have taken place within literature itself. But first it will invite you to think about reading and writing in your own life.

Response

Why have you chosen to study literature? Do you enjoy reading? Do you experience any difficulties when you read? If so, what are they? What kinds of texts do you read most often? What kind of texts do you like? Do you enjoy writing? What kinds of writing do you currently undertake on a regular basis? Do you experience any difficulties when you write? If so, what are they? What kind of writing do you like to undertake? How important is reading in your life? How important is writing to you? Do you value one more highly than the other?

If you take a moment to look back, you may find that a division between reading and writing was established in your early childhood. Reading is an activity that has traditionally been more visible at home. Perhaps a family member read you a bedtime story or encouraged you to look at picture books. You may remember parents reading a magazine or newspaper in their leisure time. Your strongest early memories of writing, meanwhile, may well be associated with school. In her survey, *Literacy in American Lives* (2001), Deborah Brandt found that parents often lacked the confidence to tutor their offspring in writing, although they might have assisted or initiated the process of learning to read. She found that the parents' own writing was associated with employment, probably occurring outside the home, or with chores: writing shopping lists or paying bills. She found that where writing was nurtured at home, it was often connected to loss and sadness: for example, children wrote letters to a parent who was absent through separation, incarceration or war. In summary, she found reading had connotations of warmth and community within the home, while writing was associated with secrecy (hidden diaries expressing angst or sadness) and even chastisement. From their handwriting to their verbal expression, people remembered their writing as receiving harsh judgement at school. It was sometimes even a source of displeasure at home: a surprising number of interviewees had been punished as infants for scrawling rude words on books and walls. Although Brandt's survey was carried out relatively recently, it is possible that from this point forwards, the responses of her interviewees would be more positive, certainly different. The explosion of new technologies such as the World Wide Web and mobile phones has already changed approaches to writing, and that writing (typing?) has become more visible in leisure time. Sending text messages to friends on mobile phones, joining chat rooms and sending emails are ways in which relaxed and informal writing practices have been introduced into the home and to some extent employed by family members of all ages.

Response

Here is an abbreviated version of the issues that Brandt asked her interviewees to consider. It is an extremely rewarding process to take time to reflect upon the role that reading and writing have played and will play in your life. If you have the opportunity to discuss your answers with other people in a seminar, it would be productive to consider how responses are affected by demographic factors such as age, gender, race, place of birth and childhood home, type of education, occupation of parents, or even grandparents.

Childhood memories

- Earliest memories of seeing other people writing and reading
- Earliest memories of self writing/reading
- Earliest memories of anyone teaching you to write/read
- Places, organisations, people and materials associated with writing/reading

Writing and reading in school

- Earliest memories of writing/reading in school
- Kinds of writing/reading done in school
- Memories of evaluation and assignments

Writing and reading with peers

- Memories of writing and reading to/with friends

Influences

- Memories of people who had a hand in your learning to write or read
- Significant events in the processes of learning to read and write

The prompts above have asked you to recollect memories associated with learning to write and read, and literacy in your childhood; the sections below are concerned with estimations of your current and future values.

Purposes

- What are the purposes for which you currently write and read? List as many as you can. Do you anticipate that they will change in the future?

Values

- Do you value writing more than reading, or vice versa, or equally? Why? Do you think that this estimation will change in the future? Why?

Adaptation reproduced by permission of Cambridge University Press and the author

The notes that you have made in consideration of these points should make explicit the attitudes to writing and reading that you hold and that will inevitably have an impact upon the work that you do at university. Have your responses uncovered any ways of thinking that have surprised you? Have they revealed areas of confidence or anxiety relating to the subject and discipline of literature? Are your responses similar to those of your peers? You might find that some of your views are socially entrenched rather than just the result of individual experience.

Let us now move from contemplation of your personal story to a short overview of the history of literacy in the West.

1.4 A *very* brief history of writing and reading

For Brandt, the anecdotes of children scribbling profanities that she recorded illustrate a point of difference between reading and writing. She suggested that, even in infancy, writing is a way of expressing independence. It can be a more visible way of showing individuality, identity or hostility, while reading and being read to are two ways in which we are socialised into community. It is a commonplace now to say that fairy tales induct children into societal norms and codes of behaviour: don't go off with strangers (say *Little Red Riding Hood* and *Hansel and Gretel*); only marriage to a man of status can lift a woman out of servitude (*Cinderella*) or awaken her sexual desire (*Sleeping Beauty*). Both reading and writing are subject to control (books can be banned or their access restricted for certain groups), but the activity of writing has a more rebellious reputation than the seemingly passive pastime of reading. Writing is regarded as more potent, more dangerous than its quiet sibling, reading – think of graffiti. And we only need to consider the historical and religious reasons for learning to read to find the origins of this formula. Reading was taught to enable access to the scriptures. It was revered as a transport to salvation and until the late eighteenth century, in Britain, it might surprise you to know, reading was taught as an activity quite distinct from writing. When it began to be taught, writing was regarded with hostility and suspicion by some factions of the Church for being vocational and assisting upward social mobility, while reading was encouraged (among social elites) because it connected solely with devotional practice. Writing was considered a literally dirty activity, with messy inks etc., which was especially unsuitable for women and girls. It was seen as a secular practice that interfered with the pious transaction of accessing God's word through reading and with the social order (by enabling ascendancy through vocational achievement). In the 1830s, Wesleyan Methodists even formed an anti-writing movement to try and stop the advent of these ill side-effects.

You can see then that a clear opposition was established between these two fundamentally linked activities: on the one hand, reading was clean and pious, and on the other, writing was dirty and secular.

Response

Can you trace any links between these attitudes to the components of literacy and your own, or those held by others in contemporary society?

But even reading was initially a circumscribed activity. In the very early days of textual reproduction, the only scribes were clerics, who painstakingly and often beautifully transcribed the scriptures in Latin. The first book ever to be printed was a Bible, also in Latin (by Johann Gutenberg in the 1450s in Mainz, Germany); the Catholic Church and then Church of England considered it a heresy to produce a Bible in a vernacular language (that is, the spoken language of the people, such as English, rather than the clerical language of Latin, which itself relied upon translations from Hebrew). But this authority had always met with resistance: in the 1380s, John Wycliffe (1320s–84) produced a Bible in English, because he believed it should be available to all Christians. The Heresy Act of 1401 decreed it an offence for anyone other than a priest to read the Bible. So, for the majority of the population, the barrier to direct Biblical knowledge was double: they could not read and neither could they understand Latin. In the early sixteenth century, William Tyndale (1494–1536), a gifted linguist and theologian, also believed that God's word should be available to everyone without the filter of priestly interpretation. He produced the first copies of the New Testament in English (1525–6), but not only did the Church burn these books upon discovery, possession continued to be a crime punishable by death by fire. The Church claimed that producing the Bible in vernacular languages would leave it open to errors of transcription, but an alternative interpretation of their desire for it to remain in Latin or Hebrew is that this enabled them a high degree of power and control. It is clear, in this brief history, that from its earliest inception, literacy has been bound to power and authority. In an age when the Bible is translated into every language and the Church rampantly seeks new readers, it is hard to believe that Tyndale was burnt at the stake – allegedly upon a pile of his English Bibles – as punishment for his reformations. The Church's anxiety about reform was a fear of the disruption of the existing social order in which they were the primary holders of knowledge: they could determine who would learn to read and write and, thus, who would maintain power within society.

Until the intervention of the state into mass education in the nineteenth century, the tools of literacy were largely the privilege of the upper-class, wealthy, urban male, while the rest of society relied upon other forms of cultural transmission: sermons, songs, sayings, stories, plays and pictures. The chances of you learning to read in the seventeenth and eighteenth centuries were thus entirely dependent upon your social status, gender and location, and while oral traditions have been cherished in the popular memory, the ability to read and write has always been coveted. Literacy may have been initially widely nurtured for spreading the gospel but from the start its transformative qualities have been associated as much with social progression as with spiritual ascendancy. Being literate has always enabled access to a wider variety of more highly esteemed vocations. And this has been, perhaps unsurprisingly, a preoccupation of the characters in many literary texts. Christopher Marlowe's play of the 1590s, *Doctor Faustus*, is about a scholar who forms a pact with one of the devil's subordinates: bored by his studies, he swaps his soul for possession of boundless wisdom for twenty-four years, a pact that exchanges a limited period of supremacy in life for an eternity in hell at the end of the two dozen years. Faustus soon regrets his bargain. When he begins to repent, Mephistopheles conjures up a parade of the seven deadly sins – Pride, Covetousness, Wrath, Envy, Gluttony, Sloth and Lechery – to distract the wavering doctor. The sins are personified as human beings with Envy characterised as an impoverished urban street-trader who is jealous of those who can read; he knows that 'to be illiterate is to be excluded from clerisy, from knowledge and the capacity to make a proper living; it is, in fact, to be condemned to exclusion in the under-class' (Wheale 1). The fact that the technical term for being unable to read and write – to be illiterate – has wider and pejorative connotations is very telling in this respect. It can be a term of abuse: to call someone illiterate is to brand them stupid and the word can be used to refer to someone who is ignorant in other branches of knowledge (you could claim to be illiterate in computing, for example).

Since the beginning, then, the written and printed word has been conflated with knowledge and status. To be able to read is to be able to gain knowledge, to raise one's status and avoid the label of ignorance; it is first an *object* of education then its *means*. We can see that the privileged in society have always had easier access to the material and symbolic tools of literacy, and have been traditionally more likely to attain higher levels of education. But even despite the existence of free and compulsory schooling for all in the West in the twentieth century, it is argued that this continues to be so. The French sociologist Pierre Bourdieu (1930–) coined the phrase *cultural capital* to refer to the symbolic tools of the elite: their cultural and linguistic forms. For example, the language

of parliament and the law is not the language of the street; the kinds of literature, art, music and museums that have been traditionally esteemed in academia are not those that have been widely accessed or enjoyed by members of the
working classes. The literature, art forms and music of Asians, African-
Americans and other ethnic groups have not been conventionally studied in
Western universities (although as we shall see in chapter 2: Reading this situation is changing). Those who are already familiar with the language and
culture of society's elite clearly begin with an advantage. Indeed, Bourdieu
argues that rather than transmitting knowledge to all, universities serve to
legitimate and duplicate the values held by the powerful. Paradoxically, thus,
universities *prevent* as well as *provide* access to power. They provide access to
power but they do so on their own terms and the path of access is circumscribed. They insist upon writing in a certain way about certain subjects and
these are not the ways or interests of society's subordinates. Bourdieu and like-
minded thinkers posit a situation in which the contemporary ruling classes are
comparable to the Church of the Middle Ages in their ability to maintain
control over education.

Elsewhere, one component of this cultural stratification is referred to as the
literacy myth. The myth is that learning to read and write will always and necessarily enable access to improved employment and social status; the reality is
that there are other factors and prejudices – on grounds of race, sex, class, religion, ethnicity and sexuality, for example – that will override educational
achievements. But the power of the literacy myth continues to be irresistible.
Literacy skills are tied to identity and belonging; a pressure that has particular
resonances for people who speak a different language at home from the one
used in school or the workplace. Since the 1940s, economic migrants who have
moved to Britain and the US to fill vacancies in the labour market have been
chastised by government members for any failure to adopt the dominant
tongue, English. The recent award-winning documentary, *Spellbound* (dir. Jeff
Blitz, 2002), is about the National Spelling Bee, a popular competition in the
US, in which young people are tested on their ability to spell often unusual
and arcane words. Promotional material sells the film as 'the story of America
itself' (www.spellboundmovie.com) because so many of the competitors are
from immigrant families whose first language is not English. For them, it
declares that victory in the regional heats represents 'assimilation and achievement of the American Dream', conflating this with 'mastery of the English language'. The film corresponds to the literacy myth, promoting the idea that
immigrants will succeed and be accepted in the US if they learn not just the
vernacular variant of the language but the rarefied linguistic forms of its historical elite.

1.5 What do novels know?

One of the oldest questions asked of literature is about the kinds of knowledge it possesses in comparison to those of philosophy. The critic Michael Wood (1936–) recently gave this question a contemporary formulation, asking more specifically whether fiction can express knowledge that philosophy can't: 'What does this novel know?' If we look at the countless examples of fictional characters who long to improve themselves, from Marlowe to the present day, we can see that many literary texts are aware of the complexities connected to the desire for learning. It seems that what novels know is that knowledge is power. The strivings of impoverished or disadvantaged individuals, who crave an education to improve their chances, status, finances, sense of belonging, is in fact the subject of a huge number of novels. But it is surprising how few depict the success of such aspirations; a survey of texts that consider the desire for social advancement through education reveals that many of them know this is indeed a myth.

Here are three examples of novels that chart the changing attitudes to literacy in the nineteenth and twentieth centuries.

1.5.1 Jude the Obscure

Thomas Hardy's fiction describes the impact upon its inhabitants of England's transformation from a land-based economy to an industrial society. At the start of Hardy's thirteenth and final novel, *Jude the Obscure* (1896), an orphan, Jude Fawley, aspires to go to university, in order to become a cleric. As the title determines, however, Jude remains in ignominious rural poverty, becoming instead first a stonemason and then a cake maker; his desires for a spiritual and intellectual life are quashed by the material demands of his existence as a poor working man, and the weight of this disappointment in contrast to his lofty ambition is symbolically depicted in the nature of his first job. The body of the novel, which shocked contemporary readers, charts the misery of his life as all his ambitions are thwarted. Hardy's novels deal compassionately with the unhappiness of ordinary working lives; we are left feeling that Jude's life could and would have been so much greater had he succeeded in studying at Christminster (the fictional university of his dreams).

1.5.2 Howards End

E. M. Forster's 1910 novel *Howards End* also contrasts the spiritual and material concerns of industrial society. The dichotomy is symbolised by two middle-class families: the Wilcoxes, who run a business, thus representing the material concerns of industry and finance, and the Schlegels, who devote their lives to intellectual pursuits. Forster's famous dictat 'Only connect' was written as an epigram to this novel, suggesting that the best society is one in which material and spiritual components exist in mutual interconnection, but in fact the story of *Howards End* suggests that this benefit might not be available to all. At a concert of classical music, Helen Schlegel meets a young man who is bent on self-improvement. Leonard Bast is a clerk whose later accidental death in the novel has an enormous symbolic resonance; he is killed by a falling bookcase when visiting the Schlegels. Both *Jude the Obscure* and *Howards End* seem to work as allegories of the fact that it is impossible for the working man to break out of the strictures his class has determined for him; their protagonists sought to improve themselves spiritually and materially through education. At the end of the nineteenth century, Jude was denied access to higher learning but even though the modern city in the early twentieth century afforded Bast white-collar employment and entrance to public lectures and cultural events, his intellectual pursuits proved his downfall, association with the middle classes resulting in his demise. In Zadie Smith's contemporary reworking of the novel, *On Beauty* (2005), a further dimension of race is introduced into the ferment of ideological and class oppositions. Her version of Bast is Carl Thomas, a hoodie-wearing rapper from the wrong side of town, whose talents as a street poet are feted for their urgency and 'authenticity' but do not prevent him being excluded from studying at the university he seeks to join and being deeply patronised by its members.

1.5.3 A Scots Quair

Lewis Grassic Gibbon's (1901–35) trilogy *A Scots Quair* (published as one collection in 1946) revises the encounter with literacy for the mid-century. Like Jude, the heroine Chris Guthrie is obliged to choose between a life on the land and university, but her choice is complicated in a manner that anticipates the dilemma of many of the participants featured in *Spellbound*. For Guthrie, education and university means a symbolic (not physical) movement away from her native Scotland to England, for it necessitates an adoption of the English language as it is spoken by the English rather than the Scots; this inevitably raises issues about her sense of national identity. Indeed, the trilogy can be read as symbolising the state of Scotland and its future: how can traditional rural Scottish life be combined with university education that is predominantly in the hands of the English? The book provides one answer to its own question in its form; it combines a version of Scots that is not regional or dialectical, with innovations in style and language, demonstrating that literature and language are in the hands of all users and not only the control of a powerful and traditional elite.

Response

Can you think of other literary texts that explore the literacy myth? Do they present education as an uncomplicated means of release from poverty or deprivation? What sacrifices are characters compelled to make in return for education? How does it affect their sense of class, race, gender or national identity?

1.6 Literacy in contemporary society

We can see then that, for the individual, literacy has always been associated with improved life chances (whether real or only perceived) but of course this is only one side of the story; capitalism demands literate workers and consumers. Can you imagine your existence in Western society without being a consumer? Have you ever thought about how dependent consumerism is upon literacy? Imagine how different your purchases would be at every level if you could not read the labels, the adverts or the magazines that contain the adverts and urge consumerism? Imagine how different your social life would be if you couldn't read the outside of DVD boxes or cinema tickets. Even for those who have not engaged with the technological developments of mobile phones, email and the World Wide Web, the act of reading as a leisure activity itself has become heavily consumerised in the recent and growing popularity of book clubs, initiated by Oprah Winfrey on her show in 1996.

For employers in postindustrial society, literacy is a valuable commodity that has taken the place of precious material commodities, such as those utilised in heavy manufacturing industries and agriculture. Western economies are now dependent upon commerce and IT (information technologies) and consequently the history of employment since the mid-twentieth century has shown that it is pretty much a necessity to be able to read and write to secure work. However, as the ability to read and write has become common, so, ironically, has the skill become devalued. It is now no longer enough to be able to read and write to gain clerical employment (in an office); you must also possess computing skills, be familiar with the Internet and be able to word-process. Where once a secretary would have been employed to transcribe and type the letters of more senior figures in the offices of every kind of workplace, the advent of reliable IT means it is far quicker and more economical for every employee to do it him/herself. What this also means is that a larger group of people than ever before are expected to have high levels of literacy skills; they (you) are expected to be expert in all matters of grammar, spelling, punctuation, precisely the skills that employers commonly complain are lacking in today's school-leavers and graduates. Here is a further example of writing's association with difficulty and failure; it is distressing to see that this connection continues beyond childhood and education.

You might be surprised, however, to find that it is a sentiment that has been heard throughout history. While commentators frequently suggest that knowledge of spelling, punctuation, correct grammatical terms and constructions is in decline and is either untaught or badly taught in compulsory education, this is an opinion that has been voiced since at least the nineteenth century. In 1879, a Harvard professor, Adams Sherman Hill, spoke to schoolteachers about the low standard of written work submitted by entrants to the university. He found grave faults in both the content and technical aspects of their writing. Those that failed were 'deformed by grossly ungrammatical or profoundly obscure sentences, and some by absolute illiteracy' (Gottschalk and Hjortshoj 3). Even those that passed 'were characterized by general defects'; the 'candidate, instead of considering what he had to say and arranging his thoughts before beginning to write, either wrote without thinking about the matter at all, or thought to no purpose. Instead of [. . .] subjecting his composition to careful revision, he either did not undertake to revise at all, or did not know how to correct his errors. Evidently he had never been taught the value of previous thought or subsequent criticism' (*ibid.*). We will consider Hill's advice for successful writing at length in our next chapters but here we are drawing attention to the strange fact that authoritative figures are always pronouncing that standards of writing are in decline. This complaint has been particularly loud at times of social change and increasing student numbers. Some people feel that it masks an ideological opposition to the expansion of higher education. Every time governments seek to increase the numbers of students going on to university and thus every time work is being done to involve more people from outside society's elites in further education, the accusation is made that these are people who are not capable of it, and will not benefit from it. Others have responded more creatively, developing innovative textbooks, courses and pedagogies to assist those who arrive at university not already in possession of the requisite 'cultural capital'. Hill himself wrote three writing textbooks. In 1966, tutors from the UK joined their US counterparts at a groundbreaking conference at Dartmouth College, New Hampshire, to spearhead an ongoing campaign of international collaboration in the teaching of English at university; their subsequent research and meetings grew to incorporate members from Australia, Canada, New Zealand and South Africa.

Earlier, I touched upon the fact that writing is regarded as more potent and potentially rebellious than reading. Some social commentators, like Bourdieu and Brandt, suggest that it is precisely because of these 'latent powers' that writing must be and is controlled. In other words, just as the sixteenth-century Church didn't want the Bible to be available to all in order to control its interpretation, so today's elites and authorities might stand to lose if everyone felt confident about, or attained, their full power of expression.

Response

Have you ever felt inhibited by the styles of writing practised at school or university? What are and have been the pressures upon you to be a 'good' writer? What does being a 'good' writer mean? Do you think that some formal modes of writing are more accessible to certain groups in society? Do you think that writing can be a subversive act?

I also suggested earlier that in this book I would not discuss aspects of writing in isolation from their context. Here is an example of how context shapes not just the style but can instil anxiety about writing. Consider the difference between writing a text message or email to a friend and composing an essay for a tutor at university. It is probable that the former usually feels less constricted than the latter. This is not because the friendly missives are free of stylistic conventions – they are entirely governed by abbreviations, symbols and a manner that would be incomprehensible to someone from an earlier time – but because these codes are defined by you and your peers and not academics in positions of authority. In other words you are more familiar with the stylistic conventions and abbreviations of the written word in your everyday life and your communications are composed from a position of equality. Furthermore, you are not being assessed on them, your future does not depend upon them; with the long tradition of fees in the US and their more recent introduction in the UK, it might be argued that this anxiety is all the greater given that your future economic success and ability to stay solvent will depend upon your academic achievement (the modern equivalent of Marlowe's lowly oyster seller?). This book will explore the conventions of academic writing but it will also try to find ways to counteract the fear of writing for those who are in power; it will present ways of questioning what you read and how you write; perhaps it might even encourage you to question why the essay has achieved dominance as a form in higher education.

1.7 Stories, narrative and identity

In *A Scots Quair*, Chris Guthrie was troubled by the thought of the Anglicisation that higher education would inevitably entail. Her Scottish accent and vocabulary would have been unacceptable at university. For her, education meant deeply compromising or even abandoning her Scottish identity. Acceptance into a particular community was not the goal that Guthrie sought from her education, unlike, we are led to believe, some of the participants in *Spellbound*. The challenge to identity, welcome or feared, is an experience shared by many who are obliged to conform to the linguistic demands of writing at university. This is something that we shall consider in the next chapter. For the literature student, the challenge can be even more striking since the subject of study is the questioning of the stories and narratives that we read and tell, which are implicated in the very construction of our personal and national identities.

In its broadest sense, a **narrative** is an account of a sequence of events, real or fictional. This definition seems to designate **stories** as a subset of the larger group called narrative – for story seems to imply a fiction – but the two terms are used interchangeably: if you look up story and narrative in a dictionary you'll find that each is used in the other's definition and that a clear demarcation that aligns one to the realm of truth and the other to fiction cannot be made. The idea that narratives are a ubiquitous part of all life, not just in explicit actions of fictional storytelling, arose from Structuralist theory (see chapter 2: Reading), in which representations of history were understood to be constructed in accordance with particular ideologies. The French philosopher Jean-François Lyotard (1924–98) introduced the phrase **grand narrative** to describe the ideologically shaped, overarching religious and political narratives that laid claim to the truth; such narratives only serve to *legitimise* rather than *explain* their authority.

The original meaning of a **story** can be inferred from the longer word 'history'; it was an account of a real incident that had happened in the past and was thus believed to be true. This meaning does bear some relation to the ways that we commonly use the word today; for example, if we congratulate someone on an anecdote they have amused us with, we might say, 'That's a good story', not implying that it is a fabrication but that the narrator has impressed us with her or his skills of recounting the episode. The emphasis upon the fact that a story must be told, it must have a teller (a narrator) who is shaping the subject and the order of events, implies of course an audience, one or more, for whom the story is recounted. Conversely, these skills of narrative construction may be precisely what leads to another everyday use of the word 'story' to denote an account that has been highly elaborated and is thus suspected of being untrue; to be accused of telling a story in court or of being a storyteller is to be charged with lying. This slipperiness of delineating between the truth and fabrication in recounted events, precisely because they are recounted, the fact that story and narrative are used synonymously, contributed to the challenge made by Lyotard *et al.* to monopolised versions of truth-telling.

Further reading

For an overview of what narrative is and how it is constructed you should read H. Porter Abbott's *The Cambridge Introduction to Narrative*; Martin Mcquillan has compiled an anthology of writings upon narrative and narratology (the study of narrative) by the key theorists from Plato (427–327 BC) to Homi K. Bhabha (1949–) in *The Narrative Reader*; for an account of the development of narrative theory see Mark Currie's *Postmodern Narrative Theory*.

In his helpful introduction to the expansive subject of stories, Richard Kearney says: 'Every life is in search of a narrative' (Kearney 4). Everyone seeks a story that will give meaning and purpose to the baffling unpredictability of existence, and, not coincidentally, the structure of life is similar to that of most stories in having a beginning, a middle and an end. Kearney's phrase (in isolation) could be read as implying that the pursuit is an individual one, but of course, as we have seen, the search for a narrative that will give meaning is quite likely to involve a story shared by many. A narrative that gives meaning might be a grand narrative, a shared religious doctrine or a national narrative; the promoters of *Spellbound* seemed to share a very conventional American narrative, for example: that of the American dream celebrating the idea that everyone, regardless of origin, can be a success in the US, and the notion that the country was indeed built on the strength of the immigrant work ethic. But even if your meaningful narrative is not a grand narrative, or not so widely documented, it is in another sense likely to be shared, not least because you desire, compose or tell it with another person in mind. The fact that we seek narratives at every level of our lives has led to the designation of the human race as *homo fabulans*, 'the tellers and interpreters of narrative' (Currie 2). As communities and as individuals, narratives are how our identities are constructed.

Towards the end of this chapter, then, we have spent some time thinking about how stories and narratives shape us, our communities, societies and nations. We'll continue to consider them, and what happens to us when we read them, in the next chapter. We have also introduced some terminology relating to the higher education system and the institutions where your learning and reading are now taking place. In chapters 3 and 4 we'll move on to consider arguments and essays, the dominant modes of discussion at university, the ways that we will consider and write about stories.

Works cited

Abbott, Porter H. *The Cambridge Introduction to Narrative*. Cambridge: Cambridge University Press, 2002.

Bennett, Andrew and Nicholas Royle. *Introduction to Literature, Criticism and Theory*. 3rd ed. Harlow: Longman, Pearson Education, 2004.

Brandt, Deborah. *Literacy in American Lives*. Cambridge: Cambridge University Press, 2001.

Bourdieu, Pierre. *The Inheritors: French Students and their Relation to Culture*. 1964. Trans. R. Nice. Chicago: University of Chicago Press, 1979.

Cuddon, J. A. *Dictionary of Literary Terms and Literary Theory*. Penguin Reference. 1977. Revised C. E. Preston. London: Penguin, 1999.

Currie, Mark. *Postmodern Narrative Theory*. Houndmills: Palgrave, 1998.

Forster, E. M. *Howards End*. 1910. London: Penguin, 1989.

Gibbon, Lewis Grassic. *A Scots Quair*. 1946. London: Polygon, 2006.

Gottschalk, Katherine and Keith Hjortshoj. *The Elements of Teaching Writing: A Resource for Instructors in All Disciplines*. Boston and New York: Bedford/St Martin's, 2004.

Hardy, Thomas. *Jude the Obscure*. 1896. London: Penguin, 1994.

Kearney, Richard. *On Stories*. Thinking in Action. London: Routledge, 2002.

Lentricchia, Frank and Thomas McLaughlin, eds. *Critical Terms for Literary Study*. 2nd ed. Chicago: University of Chicago Press, 1995.

Littlewood, Ian. *The Literature Student's Survival Kit: What Every Reader Needs to Know*. Oxford: Blackwell Publishing, 2005.

Lyotard, Jean-François. *The Postmodern Condition: A Report on Knowledge*. 1979. Trans. Geoffrey Bennington and Brian Massumi. Manchester: Manchester University Press, 1984.

Macey, David. *Dictionary of Critical Theory*. Penguin Reference. London: Penguin 2000.

Marlowe, Christopher. *Doctor Faustus, A- and B- Texts*. Eds. David Bevington and Eric Rasmussen. Oxford: Clarendon Press, 1995.

Mcquillan, Martin, ed. *The Narrative Reader*. London and New York: Routledge, 2000.

Smith, Zadie. *On Beauty*. London: Hamish Hamilton, 2005.

Spellbound. Dir. Jeff Blitz. Metrodome Distribution. 2002.

Wheale, Nigel. *Writing and Society: Literacy, Print and Politics in Britain 1590–1660*. London and New York: Routledge, 1999.

Wood, Michael. *Literature and the Taste of Knowledge*. Cambridge: Cambridge University Press, 2005.

Chapter 2

Reading

2.1 Writing as reading?

> That's the thing about books. They're alive on their own terms. Reading is like travelling with an argumentative, unpredictable good friend. It's an endless open exchange.   (Ali Smith 2)

> [Woolf] explores the way reading – whether the reading of texts or the semiotic reading of other people from their appearance – involves bridging or otherwise negotiating gaps in information, reconstructing from hints, 'not exactly what is said, nor yet entirely what is done' (*Jacob's Room* 24) to create something of greater consistency, of great constancy, in the process of 'making a whole'.   (Briggs 5)

> In effect, it is impossible to interpret a work, literary or otherwise, for and in itself, without leaving it for a moment, without projecting it elsewhere than upon itself. Or rather, this task is possible, but then the description is merely a word-for-word repetition of the work itself. It espouses the forms of work so closely that the two are identical. And, in a certain sense, every work constitutes its own best description.   (Todorov 4)

In the last chapter we considered the reputation of reading as a rather passive activity without the rebellious reputation of its partner in literacy, writing. But a paradox arises out of the multiple meanings of the word 'reading', particularly its status as a synonym for interpretation. Almost as often as we use the verb 'to read' to refer to the activity of understanding the black marks on a page, we use it to mean an appraisal or opinion of a situation, an event or another visual form such as a film. A palm reading may be one of the most extreme versions of this kind of translation, taking the inscrutable landscape of an upturned hand and identifying character traits or future happenings, but in fact every reading to a greater or lesser degree is an act of personalised interpretation. In the context of our discussion of the relationship between reading and writing, it's amusing and perplexing to consider the paradox that someone's reading of a text or a situation is quite likely to be a written account, in a critical text or a newspaper, for instance. A reading can be a writing; a writing can be a reading.

It was a key premise of mine that writing down notes and thoughts as you read can help you clarify your reading, your understanding. All acts of interpretation are the processes of recognising signs and then ordering these signs into familiar narratives. The act of reading text is the act of interpreting the black marks you see on a page, first into words and sequences of language and then into a whole story or meaningful sequence of events. But we spend our lives constantly decoding other signs, other semiotic systems (that is, of signs or symbols) outside language, as Julia Briggs in her discussion of the novelist and critic Virginia Woolf (1882–1941) points out above. (The title of Briggs's book, *Reading Virginia Woolf*, puns on several meanings of the verb; she is reading Woolf's writings; she is most probably interpreting Woolf the woman through her writings; and she is describing the readings, in all forms, that Woolf herself undertook.) Briggs notes that Woolf was often concerned 'to pursue analogies between the process of "reading people"' and reading texts. The relatively recent advent of train travel was one occasion of modern life that afforded chance encounters with strangers, for Woolf. In one of her most famous essays 'Character in Fiction' (1924) she imagines the life of 'Mrs Brown', a woman sitting opposite her in a carriage, surmising a story for her from, among other things, her anxious expression and her threadbare but spotless garments. This is a further variation on the idea of *homo fabulans*; humans cannot help but fabricate a story for the briefly glimpsed stranger or newly made acquaintance, built around the bones of a snatch of overheard conversation or a study of facial expression and clothing. Woolf suggests that the process of reading a text is similar; the reader supplies the missing gaps in the narrative to supplement the tantalising glimpses that are provided. You might feel that a published story reaches us so tightly bound that there are no gaps to fill but consider the details that you inevitably supply: in *Jane Eyre* exactly how did the plain protagonist look? (We sometimes become aware of our own interpretations when others are offered; consider the displeasure television and film adaptations often arouse.) What happened to Mr Danvers (indeed, if there ever was one) in *Rebecca*? In *Pride and Prejudice* did Darcy and Elizabeth Bennet live happily ever after?

A contemporary novelist, Ali Smith, likens a book to a person, here an argumentative friend, who will tirelessly challenge your first interpretation, each time you reread. She seems to present reading as a fray that you will inevitably return to in the endless attempt to refine and define your understanding. Neither of these accounts – by Woolf and Smith – makes reading appear a passive and docile activity. Instead it is a process in which the text is locked in a

relationship with the reader, dependent upon him or her to provide the interpretation, plug the gaps.

2.2 A love of literature

But it is more common to imagine the relationship as one of unrequited love,
in which the text is revered by the reader who can only stand back and admire.
It is more common to imagine the text is complete, already whole, and not, as
Woolf suggests, a patchwork of material and gaps to which the reader will contribute his or her understanding to construct a whole. Readers can feel happier
expressing straightforward approval for a text that is 'good' and disdain for one
that is 'bad' than having this kind of conversation with it. Conversation
demands an equality of relationship that readers often don't feel that they
share with a writer or with the text. In this more common understanding,
reading and writing are once more distinct, as are the text and the reader. And
this distinction, which allows only for the affirmation of the value of a text in a
deferential manner, totally inhibits your readings, your writing about it; it
doesn't provide much to say. It also implies a straightforward affiliation with
the original text, which the Bulgarian-born critic, Tzvetan Todorov (1939–),
stating what Woolf and Smith imply, has claimed is in any case impossible.
Unless we reproduce the text word-for-word in our writings or discussion of it,
we offer an opinion, an interpretation. It is impossible to describe a text
without in some way reducing it (abbreviating it, refusing or not seeing possible ambiguities) and in some way adding to it (inevitably bringing to it our
own opinions, beliefs and ideas with which to fill the gaps). The first chapter of
this book mentioned that we grow up with stories and discussed historical and
cultural attitudes towards reading and writing; the next two are about questioning those stories, making our interpretations explicit.

   The three main topics for discussion in this chapter connect your experience
as a new English undergraduate with the history of the discipline of Literature
in the twentieth century itself. They are in some ways about the loss of self. One
of the conceptions of the subject of English, of studying texts, is that there are
no right or wrong answers. The synonymous status of reading with interpretation that I have discussed above seems to support the conviction that a literary
work can be construed in an almost infinite number of ways (as long as these
construals are properly backed up). There might be as many interpretations of
a text as there are people to read it, according to this view. However, when you
are asked to submit your interpretation in writing, most probably as an essay, it
is likely that you will be asked for something more analytical than a personal

opinion, and be required instead to employ a critical theory, a systematic analytical framework, a way of thinking that has been defined by someone else. This can feel closer to an extermination of personality and individuality than a celebration of them, as you are asked to negotiate a multiverse of isms and schools, each with its own distinct terminology and political affiliations, social positioning and methodological discussion.

This feeling of loss of self might be further exaggerated in the process of acquiring a properly academic voice. The pressure to leave your own voice behind for the purposes of academic study is an interesting one, considering that the most heinous offence in the academy is the complete loss of one's own voice – plagiarism. While your tutors will encourage a kind of analytical depersonalisation, a distancing from the text in order to scrutinise it, this occurs within strictly defined limits: the adoption of a new **discourse** is rewarded, but the wholesale adoption of someone else's voice is penalised. This paradox is undeniably one of the greatest sources of difficulty among students, but it does define a kind of philosophical problem about the self that goes to the heart of writing about literature: namely, a kind of contradiction between the loss of self and the maintenance of self that is required by the keepers of academic literary criticism. As we shall see in this chapter, it also provides an entry into interesting but problematic discussion of how originality is prized in our society. The discussion of these issues intends to offer a practical guide to the problems of reading and writing, and writing as reading in an English degree.

2.3 The discipline of English

At school the study of literature can still involve a close reading or 'practical criticism' of a novel, play or poem without much or any recourse to external material. Practical criticism is the method of analysing a poem, in isolation from the circumstances of its production, developed by I. A. Richards (1893–1979) in the 1920s. He felt that concentration upon 'the words on the page', the technical aspects of the ways verse creates effects, would result in meaningful judgements upon whether a poem was intrinsically 'good' or simply reputedly so. The methodology of practical criticism seeks coherence in images, themes and patterns of language. Richards and his colleagues felt that this practice was 'scientific' and led to objective value judgements. He was part of a group of lecturers at Cambridge University who played a crucial role in the development of the discipline of English Literature and whose methodology influenced the critical practices of the New Critics, John Crowe Ransom (1888–1974) and Cleanth Brooks (1906–94) and their colleagues in the US.

Their 'scientific' examination of literature asserted a hierarchy of texts, those that held universal meaning and significance through aesthetic form and those deemed too formulaic to warrant academic scrutiny. The first, revered, group of texts is often referred to as the **literary canon**.

The name and, to some extent, the idea of an authoritative list of poetry, plays and prose fiction originates in the ecclesiastical Canons: a list of texts believed to inspire divine revelation, ratified by James I in 1603. So while the literary canon designated well-known authors, such as Geoffrey Chaucer (1343?–1400) and William Shakespeare (1564–1616), as numinous, it simultaneously deemed all kinds of genre fiction – romances, thrillers, science fiction etc. – as unlikely to produce spiritual enlightenment. When writing about what should be included in a university literature course, Q. D. Leavis (1906–81), a literary critic and student of Richards at Cambridge, dismissed the enormous public appetite for such popular fictions as more akin to a 'drug habit' than a cerebral pursuit (7). Thus, in the early establishment of the English Literature degree, a rigid division was erected between high and popular culture, and, with the exception of some modernist texts (the poetry of T. S. Eliot (1888–1965), Joseph Conrad's novels (1857–1924)), between pre-twentieth-century and contemporary writing. For F. R. Leavis (1895–1978), the enormously influential proponent of close reading – and husband of Q. D. Leavis – the evaluative practice of literary criticism, as well as reading canonical literature itself, could be a civilising experience paralleling that of traditional religious observance. Leavis believed in establishing a small core of texts to be taught in schools and universities in Britain and the Commonwealth that would have a 'civilising' impact. He aimed to restore

> to this country an educated public that shall be intelligent, conscious of its responsibility, qualified for it and influential – such a public as might affect decisively the intellectual and spiritual climate in which statesmen and politicians form their ideas, calculate, plan and perform.
>
> (F. R. Leavis, *English Literature* 29–30)

Always controversial, the idea that the canon is a list of great works based on objective scientific methodological analysis has been challenged vigorously during the last twenty-five years.

In 1948 F. R. Leavis ordained Jane Austen (1775–1817), George Eliot (1819–80), Henry James (1843–1916) and Joseph Conrad as the 'great English Novelists' in *The Great Tradition*. Although two of Leavis's great novelists are women (George Eliot was a pseudonym), the canon, as a damning epithet deems it, is largely composed of works by 'dead white men'. And, somewhat ironically, in fact *The Great Tradition* considers only one woman, for under the guise of the greatest accolade, Leavis omits discussion of Austen because he claims she deserves a full-length study of her own (F. R. Leavis, *Great Tradition* 1). Nor does the canon include much literature by members from different ethnic or social backgrounds. Critics argue, therefore, that belonging to the canon signifies not a text's intrinsic worth or 'moral seriousness' as Leavis claimed, but its perceived reflection of dominant belief systems, that the universal 'truths', so fervently sought and revered by the New Critics, are simply not universal at all. The canon is criticised both for the exclusivity of its membership and its attendant interpretive practice that discovers only the coherent reflection of societal norms, authoritatively asserting a unified and yet socially stratified society. Other writings are unpublished or ignored and other readings of canonical texts – ones that find incoherence or subversion – are suppressed. Since the Cambridge–New Critical tradition, however, critics have responded in different ways to the literary canon. Some seek to reshape it to include marginalised texts; some to dismantle or ignore it by studying popular culture or other writings instead; some to read canonical texts in different ways. Others hope to form new alternative literary canons, for example, of African-American writings. The literary canon has undergone many reshapings since its sixteenth-century origins; it seems fated to an evolving, enduring and yet negotiated permanence.

The canon's resilience is unsurprising given the claim of its detractors: that it authorises the values of society's elite. Its advocates do indeed comprise the powerful. Prestigious scholars follow the Leavisite tradition, fanfaring declarations of great works. In 1994, Harold Bloom (1930–), professor at Yale, asserted the legitimacy of the Western Literary Canon, controversially defending it against the 'School of Resentment', critics and journalists who seek to 'overthrow the Canon in order to advance their supposed (and nonexistent) programs for social change' (Bloom 4). Shunning an academic audience, Bloom intended his book *The Western Canon* to restore 'the romance of reading' (Bloom 15) to the general public (518). Meanwhile, in Britain the successive Conservative governments of the 1980s and 1990s closed down developments in the compulsory education of 7- to 16-year-olds that introduced non-canonical texts, instead reinstating classics that apparently encouraged an English nationalism; they saw 'literature teaching as part of the continuance and inculcation of "heritage" – a heritage [that is] mythically "English" rather than European, rather than international, rather than Scottish, Welsh or Irish' (Andrews and Mitchell 59). Many students still arrive at university expecting to study only well-known texts by well-known authors (even if the term 'canon' is new to them) and with the exception of some segregated (and tokenistic?) courses on African-American or Irish or Women's Writing, this may well be what they will do. Q. D. Leavis's disdain for genre fiction may be disregarded in some departments that offer courses on things like Crime Fictions but the belief that certain texts can be deemed more valuable than others, which is connected to morality and can be somehow determined through examination of formal qualities, has remained powerful in the minds of governments, the ruling bodies of schools and perhaps the general public. But wherever you position yourself in relation to the literary canon, unreflective admiration for its texts will no longer suffice as academic literary study.

Genre A type or category of text usually defined by form or theme. The three main genres of literature as defined by form are novels, poetry and plays, but these broad categories are further subdivided by structural or subject criteria into subgenres, for example, in poetry, sonnets and elegies (terms that have both formal and thematic implications), in drama, tragedy and comedy (most immediately recognised by the content of their endings). The term **genre fiction** meanwhile often has negative connotations; it is applied to categories of popular fiction such as science and crime fiction, distinguishing them from 'literary' fiction.

Response

- What types of texts did you expect to study on a literature course? Which authors did you anticipate reading?
- Have these expectations been met or confounded? Have you looked at genres or categories of writing (such as non-fiction, diaries or documents) that are unfamiliar to you or unexpected?
- Have you heard of the authors you are being asked to study? Are you studying any texts that don't have named or single authors?

2.4 The new English student

Since the close reading techniques established by the Cambridge School and the New Critics there has been a movement away from autonomous aesthetic judgements (with precise and universal standards for evaluating art) to cultural studies (which recognise that meanings are made contextually). Practical criticism has not been replaced by one contextual methodology but has flowered into many schools of criticism (which do still rely on practices of close reading). These forms of critical analysis can be grouped under the following very broad headings: Feminism and Gender studies; Gay, Lesbian and Queer theory; Marxism and materialism; New Historicism; Psycho-analysis; Race, Ethnic and Postcolonial theories; Reader-response theory; and Structuralism, Deconstruction and Poststructuralism. As you progress through your own study you should aim to break these down into smaller affiliations or studies of particular authors.

Schools of criticism: a *very* brief outline

Feminism and Gender studies

As Ruth Robbins in her helpful introduction to literary feminisms outlines, feminism is the political movement that explores the conflation of the condition of being female (a biological category) with being feminine (a social or cultural classification) (Robbins 6). Feminist literary theory is thus one branch of this wider political activity, broadly examining literature and linguistics as part of the culture that perpetrates the conflation. The history of Western feminism shows that a concern with the material conditions of female oppression with a focus on biological essentialism has been replaced by the recognition that historical and other contextual factors show important distinctions (of race and class, for example) between women and women's experiences. Recently, the work of critics – most notably Judith Butler – has decried the notion of female essentialism, arguing instead that in being socially constructed, gender roles are performative: that is, they are culturally adopted rather than intrinsic qualities of the body. This theory of gender studies is fundamental to the following critical school that also latterly understands all kinds of identity as socially constructed.

Gay, Lesbian and Queer theory

As with feminism, the history of criticism pertaining to homosexuality first celebrated a common identity as a political movement, and then fragmented it through later thinking that discovered and endorsed pluralism, identi*ties*. Texts were analysed to discover attitudes to homosexuality just as feminist critics examined canonical works for evidence of a dominant patriarchal ideology. Since the 1970s, however, the political gay liberation movement that argues for assimilation through the equality of rights between homo- and heterosexuals (to marry and parent, for example) has developed coterminous with an attack upon an understanding of sexual and gender identity as biologically determined. Michel Foucault's *History of Sexuality, Volume I* (first published in English in 1979) popularised the view that all identity is provisional, historically contingent and socially constructed. Unlike gay assimilation, queer theory celebrates transgression and difference, repudiating the values – especially of family and monogamy – of the 'straight' world. While gay and lesbian theories examine sexual difference as it relates to male and female gender respectively, queer theory attempts to analyse sexual difference at some distance from gender or removed from it entirely. Eve Kosofsky Sedgwick (1950–) developed a theory of 'queer performativity' and established the notion of homosociality, the social bonding between men that provides for them a privileged access to power from which women are excluded.

Marxism and materialism

These approaches are inspired by the philosophy of historical and political economy of Karl Marx (1818–83). Marx argued that human behaviour is governed by the hierarchical power relations of capitalist society, which are hidden from consciousness. The crudest formula of this understanding of ideology posits a relationship between the economic base (the modes of production of material life) and the superstructure of social, legal, political and intellectual forms that emerge from it. Although Marx did not provide a critical framework for analysing literature, those who followed him, notably Georg Lukács (1885–1971), Walter Benjamin (1892–1940), Theodor Adorno (1903–69), Raymond Williams (1921–88) and Terry Eagleton (1943–) analyse literature as a product, although with strikingly different results, especially when considering the possibilities of Realism as a force of enlightenment or conservatism, the relationship between text and history and the possibility of the text changing history. For Fredric Jameson (1934–) ideology is literature's raw material; like Mikhail Bakhtin (1895–1975), he argues that the possibilities of mixing genres afforded by the modern novel allow for a dialogue between different discourses.

New Historicism

Stephen Greenblatt (1943–), Renaissance and Shakespeare scholar, coined this term that has come to refer to a set of cultural practices seeking to prioritise the historical and cultural context rather than solely text-based readings of literature. Originating in the US in the 1980s, the movement has focused upon the Renaissance but does not seek to reinstate history as an entity separate from the text, instead exploring all kinds of texts as belonging to an indivisible system of influence. In this, as with the approaches above, they demonstrate the influence of Foucault. New Historicists recognise that current interpretation of historical texts is equally victim to contemporary ideology and, as such, readers can never understand the text as it was understood at the time of production. H. Aram Veeser authored a helpful introduction to his collection of New Historicist writings in 1989; with Catherine Gallagher, Greenblatt published *Practicing New Historicism*, a reader that vividly demonstrates the possibilities of this approach with reference to texts from the fifteenth century to Dickens.

Psychoanalysis

Sigmund Freud (1856–1939) can be credited as the father of both the practice of psychoanalysis and psychoanalytical literary criticism. For Freud, the practice of psychoanalysis is a scientific discipline concerned to investigate the unconscious and to treat the neuroses that arise out of the suppression of unconscious desires; his theories were drawn in part from literary texts, most famously *Oedipus Rex*. Although the unconscious itself can never be penetrated, the material of the dreams and texts that it shapes can be analysed to try and gain some sense of what it comprises. The focus of psychoanalytical literary practice is thus, very broadly speaking, to discover hidden meanings and subtexts that were not in the conscious mind of the writer (not necessarily pertaining to the individual author but to the specificity of his or her cultural background). Although the precise details of Freud's psychoanalytical concepts were variously criticised and discredited, the discovery of the existence of the unconscious was to shape the twentieth century in incalculable ways. Psychoanalysis continues to be practised and its theories, which were developed by Freud himself and others including Jacques Lacan (1901–81), persist. Significant advancements in psychoanalysis arose out of feminist discussion; writers in the 1970s were divided in finding the practice either masculinist or as offering an alternative order to patriarchy. Literature students will find a compelling reading of the poetry of Sylvia Plath in the work of contemporary psychoanalytical and feminist critic Jacqueline Rose (1949–).

Race, Ethnic and Postcolonial theories

This umbrella heading incorporates work undertaken throughout the world within the field of race and ethnicity. Challenging the notions of racial essentialism, and inferiority, that were established in late nineteenth-century and early-twentieth-century European discourses of anthropology and ethnography (forming a 'scientific' rationale for colonialism), recent theory has analysed race as an ideological construct. In terms of literature it has sought to destabilise the canon, the dominant readings that prize European and white American traditions above African, African-American, Caribbean, all non-Western works and styles. In America, the theorising of the oral culture and black vernacular of slave communities by Henry Louis Gates (1950–) has been deeply influential; Barbara Smith (1946–) called for a black feminist literary criticism; bell hooks (1953–) challenged the 'ethnocentric white values' which led to the prioritising of gender over race in white feminist theory. Confronting colonial discourse, the work of Homi Bhabha (1950–) analyses the ways that literatures and canons contribute to nation-building; nations being, to employ the phrase of Benedict Anderson (1936–), 'imagined communities' built on a collective belief in shared history and community rather than racial purity. Instead, through discussion of hybridity, Bhabha argues that the theory of Orientalism associated with Edward Said (1935–2003) repeats the construct that it seeks to critique, of the West and the Orient, an Other only defined by and in relation to the West. Gayatri Chakravorty Spivak (1942–), like Bhabha, engages with the emphasis placed on textuality and representation by Jacques Derrida (1930–2004) to urge a 'transnational cultural studies'. Translator of Derrida, Spivak has been described as a feminist deconstructionist; her work seeks to expose the binary oppositions of men/women, first world/third world as Western and patriarchal constructs.

Reader-response theory

As the name suggests, this group of approaches focuses on the reader's role in interpreting the text. This is not always to say that meaning is dependent upon the reader's individual life experiences, which might generate a subjective appreciation or disapproval of a text (although some of the theory's practitioners do argue this), but that it is up to the reader to recognise the codes of a text (genre and discourse) which will establish its meaning. Meaning lies in the text but this must be completed by the reader. The key theorists of Reader-response theory are Wolfgang Iser (1926–) and Stanley Fish (1938–).

Structuralism, Deconstruction and Poststructuralism

Structuralist criticism is a highly systematic, and even scientific, approach to the analysis of literary texts. Based on the linguistics of Ferdinand de Saussure (1857–1913), and his posthumous text *Course in General Linguistics*, the fundamental belief of Structuralist critics is that the study of literature is a subset of the study of language in general, and that the critical act should focus on the underlying systems that make meaning possible. This produces a kind of analysis that is indifferent to the cultural or aesthetic value of a work of literature, but seeks instead to relate the particular form of words in a text to the structures that exist in the language system more generally, which enable the production of meaning and of literary effects. Perhaps the most significant achievements of Structuralist criticism were in narratology, or the systematic study of narrative, where a linguistic model allowed for the development of what is often referred to as a semiological study of stories and the way that they work. The Structuralist approach to semiology, based on Saussure, tends to emphasise the role of oppositions in the production of meaning, and views the binary opposition (for example, night/day, man/woman) as the basic structure that underlies the sense-making operations of language. Later developments in the Structuralist tradition are often referred to under the heading 'Deconstruction' or the more general term 'Poststructuralism'. These later developments are best thought of as critiques of the idea that you can be scientific about meaning. The idea that you can think of meaning in terms of structures is largely rejected by Poststructuralists, who emphasise instead the impossibility of a complete account of meaning. They tend to describe meaning in terms of movement, or instability, and words such as Derrida's term 'différance' point to the failure of Structuralist attempts to nail down significance with a scientific method. Poststructuralists also reject the highly language-focused approaches of linguistics, and often aim to re-establish the link between language and other forces, such as social power. To this end, the Poststructuralist will characteristically view the binary opposition as a kind of hierarchy, in which social relations and power relations are lurking. There are clear ways in which the deconstruction of literary texts, and the Poststructuralist critique of scientific values in criticism, lead directly towards the New Historicist approaches of recent decades. Derrida's first book, *Of Grammatology*, is not an easy read but Nicholas Royle has provided a recent and accessible account of his work; Hawkes and Norris provide overviews of Structuralism and Semiotics, and Deconstruction, respectively.

Further reading

Among the many introductions to literary theory, a perspicuous survey by Richard Harland, a writer of science fiction and former lecturer, stands out. Gregory Castle's *Blackwell Guide to Literary Theory* provides a timeline of theoretical texts; overviews of more key movements than I have identified above; brief biographies and bibliographies of key figures; and finally a section with theoretical readings of canonical texts such as *Ulysses* and *Midnight's Children*.

Terry Eagleton's *Literary Theory: An Introduction* has almost become a canonical text in its own right; he includes a chapter on 'The Rise of English' that analyses the development of the discipline as discussed above. Peter Barry's *Beginning Theory* is designed for English students; Jonathan Culler's *Literary Theory: A Very Short Introduction* is a clear overview that can be read in a couple of hours. Each of these guides identifies some key texts from the different critical schools for you to pursue particular interests. http://bcs.bedfordstmartins.com/virtualit/poetry/critical.html is a helpful website with an overview of each critical school and some applications to literary texts.

Like practical criticism, these theoretical outlooks have developed within English departments, transforming them along the way. At university, the novels, plays or poems on courses may no longer be canonical and may be studied as of equal value to lesser-known literary texts, diaries, letters, public documents, non-fiction. Furthermore, students are no longer expected to study them in isolation but in tandem with key texts from the schools of criticism listed above. (This is one of the reasons why the study of texts may take place now within departments or programmes called, for example, English/English Studies/Cultural Studies rather than Literature.) Instead of determining the value of a text through a close reading of its technical features, the new focus on historical and cultural placement considers the text's production and the value judgements of the society that received it. Such studies place books firmly within the 'real world'. They attempt to make explicit processes of interpretation that may have been invisible formerly. They understand books as products of and producers of ideology. However, while the romantic (and Romantic) fantasy of the divinely inspired brooding writer, sitting in his lonely garret away from the hubbub of society, has been shattered by contemporary contextualising theories, it would be a mistake to assume that the same fate has befallen the texts.

To alert students to such new ways of reading and the varieties and status of different texts, most English departments offer introductory courses in the first year. Such modules, called things like *Introduction to Criticism* and *Ways of Reading*, introduce the bewildering array of theories above (Feminism, New Historicism etc.) and give examples of the ways they can be applied to texts;

you might read the deconstruction of *Heart of Darkness*, Joseph Conrad's 1901 novella, by J. Hillis Miller (1928–), and compare this to the account given by a New Historicist such as Brook Thomas (1942–) (Murfin 206–20, 239–57). This, often brief, rather superficial introduction is intended to form the beginning of a degree-long relationship with one or more of the positions, furnishing the student with critical tools from which to analyse texts in every subsequent module. (The reality is sometimes more frustrating: after their introduction, some, or even all, of these theories are never mentioned again, leaving students to doubt their significance, revert to unreflective evaluation and gain low marks for assignments.) A further function of such modules is to ask students, 'What is a degree in English?', to raise awareness of the fact that the course that they have embarked upon may not be what they had supposed. It is a big question to ask. And especially for those students who have assumed or experienced the study of English to be about 'backing up' their assertion that a particular text is 'good'. The novelty of questions such as, 'How has this text been interpreted?', 'Why has/hasn't it been deemed canonical?' and 'Why should we read it?', and the realisation that 'Because it is good' or 'Because I like it' is not a sufficient answer, can be a deeply unsettling one for the beginning student. Here is an extract from an eloquent reflection upon this learning experience from an English student in a first semester module called *Ways of Reading*:

> From the outset of this module I have encountered confusion, a lack of understanding of some of the approaches studied so far. I am perplexed by the many different critical theories and the dilemma in applying these approaches to any given text. The different theories appear to seep into one another, much like water permeating rock. When I think I have grasped a concept, a specific critical approach, the water seems to freeze, the rock cracks and I am left with new ideas, and more exciting and intriguing approaches to ways of reading. The theories are now infiltrating every module I am currently studying, creating both more confusion and at the same time an increase in confidence.
>
> Looking at my new found confidence it appears to be inspired in many ways from my confusion, a realisation that as a student my approach to a text can also be considered and that my opinions, ideas, and thoughts can be taken into account. At first sight there appears to be no right or wrong answer, this may change as the module and my degree unfolds. The brevity of this paragraph deliberately reflects my confidence in its embryonic stage.
>
> My basic comprehension of the module plays a major part in having an understanding of the different ways of reading. Through the lectures and seminars so far it has become clear that the *Ways of Reading* module puts the correct name to approaches that I have been applying to reading (albeit unconsciously) to every text I have read, enjoyed and even hated. I have often

wondered about an author, empathised with a character and marvelled at the imagery woven into a text. I have read novels to find out more about a particular historical period and approached established literary texts, the one the canon implies we should be reading in different ways to 'trashy' novels on the best seller list. These approaches now have titles, they have theory and it is these theories that I need to learn in order to speak with conviction and clarity on future essay questions.

Ways of Reading seems to be about turning things on their head, to look at different forms of text from many different angles and calling on the reader's choices, confusion, confidence and comprehension. In conclusion I have thought about how ways of reading can be applied to any text, including my essay. I wondered about the kinds of approaches as a lecturer/reader you may use when marking this essay. This essay is anonymous but could you use *Ways of Reading* to work out who the author is? Am I male or female? Young or old? Will you look at the essay intrinsically, looking at the form, style, metaphors and imagery used or will you look at the essay extrinsically? Can you see what may have motivated me to choose this question above the other [a draft of the final assignment]? Does this essay tell you anything about me?

I can no longer detach myself from this new found knowledge, that is *Ways of Reading*, there is no going back for me now, all texts in many ways have lost their innocence. I am unable to read anything without reflecting upon the components of the module. At this point my learning experience is balanced equally between positive and negative, as the module unfolds I am convinced that the positive will outweigh the negative.

Reproduced by kind permission of Tracey Tingey

This is a meditation on the juncture faced by all beginning English under-graduates; experienced by some as a crisis. Tracey still describes 'hating' some books in her past reading but realises that from now on, as a literature student, she can no longer rely upon such opinions as a method of discussing texts. As we have seen in the last chapter, reading is part of cultural belonging. Fairy tales and storybooks are the first texts children encounter as the start of the process of socialisation into society. It is the realisation that books are part of the real world, that they are ideological products, that erects the stumbling block between old ways of reading and new. Tracey's description of this event creates a poignant moment in her conclusion when she reveals that as a result of the module, for her, all texts have lost their 'innocence'. But in fact her account, through use of the first-person pronoun ('I can no longer detach myself . . .'), discloses that she has lost her innocence as a reader. Simply liking a book is no longer enough.

In the essay, Tracey is coming to terms with four things: that an individual's views are not paramount in academic literary criticism; that taste and passion are in themselves too ideologically dense to analyse; that what has replaced literary value judgements in English studies is a multiverse of isms and schools; and that, finally, the new literature student must adopt a critical voice and negotiate a critical position within this multiverse. These precepts, regardless of whether or not they are explicitly spelt out by lecturers, meet with some resistance from freshers. The uncertainty residing at the close of the above account is tentatively resolved in optimism, 'that the positive will outweigh the negative', but there are many students whose accounts are more defiant. Tracey recognises that she has in fact practised some of the approaches unwittingly when she read in the past but now they have names and theories that she must learn 'in order to speak with conviction and clarity on future essay questions'. She feels that, although she has interrogated books in the ways that the discipline demands, she must now adopt a new discourse in order to succeed. Her own voice will not be acceptable. Other students feel that the unfamiliar literary theories are coercive, demanding agreement in ways that prevent them from expressing their own views. They object to the idea of adopting another('s) voice.

Discourse This term is traditionally used to mean a formal and extended discussion of a topic, like a sermon or a dissertation. The influence of linguistic theories of communication upon Structuralism gave it a much wider application, however; it has come to mean the language and statements used by any designated group or community, governed by conventions. Stanley Fish, an exponent of Reader-response theory and critic of Structuralism, termed these groups 'interpretive communities', whose members achieve 'literary competence' (competence in reading) through the absorption of the features of the literary discourse.

This resistance reflects both the contemporary cult of individuality that decrees self-expression paramount, and other life experiences. For the majority of students, those who begin university within a year or two of leaving school, the demand to read in a new critical way coincides with a new independence in which educational figures of authority may be something to shun, not emulate. Students may not want the university experience to simulate the power relations of the compulsory teacher/pupil relationship at school. Others may find the discourse of academic literary studies too strongly bound to the white, middle-aged, middle-class men who were involved with its inception. The imitation of their views and voices is neither desirable nor convincing. This is the problem that you will face as a beginning student: if the attempt to write in another's voice can lead to stiff and stilted writing, accusations of pretension and an unconvincing use of terminology, but reliance upon one's own voice is inadequate, then how do you read (that is, interpret and write) at university?

Response

- Have you been asked to describe your learning experience as you begin literary studies?
- How did you study literature at school? Did you undertake practical criticism or were you encouraged to explore other theories about a text's production and context?
- Have you been exposed to new ways of reading at university? What are their names? Are there critical approaches that you are particularly interested in or hostile to? Why?
- Has your own reading changed as a consequence of study at university level? How? Have you discussed this in seminars or informally with your peers?

2.5 Plagiarism: too complete a loss of self

Finding an acceptable critical voice is difficult. For some students, it is so difficult they abandon the attempt entirely and resort to using someone else's. This is one of the paradoxes of academic literary study, as I suggested in my introduction to this chapter. On the one hand, you are requested to put your own views at a distance, but if you follow this injunction entirely then you find that you have committed an offence. There is a further reason why plagiarism in literary study seems a peculiar paradox: it has an acceptable artistic corollary known as 'influence' and studied as 'intertextuality'. An essay on poetic originality by T. S. Eliot, the poet and critic, is often reduced to the aphorism: 'immature poets imitate; mature poets steal', and much critical thinking in the late twentieth century investigates the apparent impossibility of originality in creative work, while much literary fiction, poetry and drama overtly explore other texts (Eliot 13–22). The borrowing or appropriation of texts seems to be widespread but when detected in student writing it bears the criminal tag of plagiarism. Be in no doubt: whatever your attitude or practice regarding it, your lecturers are on red alert, your studies cannot help but be affected by it. From the flagrant deceit of commissioning and paying for an entire essay to the heightened anxiety that puts a stop to secondary reading altogether, one way or another your reading practices will be significantly shaped by your awareness and understanding of plagiarism. Like other critical practices, the status and occurrence of plagiarism is shaping the discipline.

The construct of plagiarism is dependent upon notions of value and originality; it is the '*wrongful* appropriation or purloining, and publication as one's own, of the ideas, or the expression of the ideas (literary, artistic, musical, mechanical, etc.) of another' [my italics] (*OED*). In a culture that prizes individuality and originality, the appropriation of another's work is seen as constituting two major crimes, theft and fraud: the theft of someone else's ideas or words and the deception of passing them off as your own. In spite of Eliot's claim, it seems there is no *rightful* appropriation. The section on plagiarism in the style guide of the MLA (Modern Language Association of America) depicts it in no uncertain terms as an enduring moral catastrophe; although 'a starving person who steals a loaf of bread can be rehabilitated, plagiarists rarely recover the trust of those they try to deceive' and if writers by profession they 'are likely to lose their jobs [. . .] suffer public embarrassment and loss of prestige' (67). It would seem that it is preferable to be a thief of objects than of expressions. The MLA quotes a *New York Times* journalist: 'we make more distinction among degrees of murder than we do among kinds of plagiarism' (Gibaldi 66). There are many paradoxes here: plagiarism is the most heinous of crimes and yet apparently widely committed; those that commit it are to be pitied, scorned, they undermine 'important public values' (*ibid.*) and yet the most respected artists openly boast of it. Although the *New York Times* journalist claimed that no categories of plagiarism are made (the word is a condemnation in itself), there are distinctions to be drawn between appropriation as an offence and the other forms borrowing can take. But perhaps there is a more important distinction to make. Although the term plagiarism is defined as the unacknowledged use of another's material it has a more precise meaning: the detected unacknowledged use of another's words. The work of successful plagiarists, like all convincing forgeries (and all great writers according to Eliot), will go, at least, unnoticed, at best, celebrated. Only those who fail are detected. In attempting to shame and frighten writers into their own voices, the author of the *MLA Handbook* (and those who share his rhetoric) appeals not then to their talent as writers but to their morality as people.

As a moral issue, then, what I call knowing plagiarism is the kind that causes widespread anger and a sense of injustice; it is perhaps the type of appropriation that is most widely understood and vilified. This is the practice of commissioning an essay, knowingly taking text directly from a website or a book, and reproducing it, without acknowledgement, as your own work. Because of the ease of 'cutting and pasting' from the web (and in some places the anonymity of submitting work electronically), the web is perceived to have increased the occurrence of plagiarism and turned it into a crime wave. Many academics are outraged by the idea of this deception and often feel personally insulted that students are trying to trick them. These plagiarists are perceived to be cunning and lazy and lecturers are therefore gratified to discover and punish their foul play. Consequently, the penalties for detected plagiarism in most universities are severe; they can range from failing the piece of work to the failure of the whole degree, depending upon the stage at which the offence was committed. (The rules and penalties enforced by your university will be published on its website and in your student handbook.)

In many ways, the construction of plagiarism as a monolithic and moral offence committed by fraudsters obfuscates serious issues. It lays the blame on the culprit and focuses attention upon its uncovering; there are conferences, websites and services dedicated to the tracking down of plagiarism. It draws attention away from the reasons why students experience anxiety about writing. It forgets the question: who can join the interpretive community of the literary discipline? It detracts from the responsibilities that academics and universities have in preventing plagiarism in the first place. It obscures the challenging questions surrounding individuality, originality and value in this society. No one believes that a degree should be gained by the unacknowledged representation of other people's work but, as we have begun to examine, sometimes the reasons why students are anxious about submitting their own words for assessment are less reprehensible than the popular understanding of plagiarism as a moral crime suggests.

There are probably two main causes of inadvertent plagiarism, which is the plagiarism that, although still an offence, might be regarded as the result of a lack of care rather than a lack of scruples: for example, when you incorporate a phrase into your essay from your notes, not remembering that it was a phrase you'd recorded from a critic or your lecture notes. Accidental plagiarism can happen when you don't establish and adhere to rigorous note-taking and writing practices (like the ones I outline below). It is easy to misremember the origins of a memorable phrase and unless you can check your writing against the original source, or your notes from it, you may imagine yourself to be its author. If you don't clearly distinguish between your own words and those of your tutor in your lecture notes then you could easily present unattributed statements in your essays. The other main cause of inadvertent plagiarism is cultural. The practice of reproducing extracts verbatim is acceptable in other environments (for example, in some workplaces it is common for elements of reports to be shared to save each member of staff having to write and rewrite standard material). Some students mistakenly believe that the practice of 'cutting and pasting' passages from website sources and synthesising it with their own work is acceptable as long as the site is listed in their bibliography, for instance. This is erroneous: no matter what the customary practices are outside higher education, nor the paradoxes of being compelled to write within a specific discourse and be original, the unacknowledged reproduction of material from websites, journals, books, lecture notes, anywhere – whether you have paid for it or not – is plagiarism and if you are found out you will be penalised. Most institutions will penalise plagiarism whether or not it is inadvertent; furthermore, it is hard to prove that your reproduction was accidental. To draw attention to your responsibility, most departments request you to sign declarations that submitted work is your own and all universities will have clear guidelines as to what constitutes plagiarism. Ignorance is no excuse; it is still your fault if you have not familiarised yourself with your university's rules and regulations. However, if your department has offered generalised written policies that you find hard to relate to your assignments, then you should ask a tutor for further guidance and, preferably, real examples.

The consequences of knowing and inadvertent plagiarism have a negative impact on university staff, students and the literary discipline itself. Some lecturers become suspicious and fixated upon the pursuit of plagiarists, who will exploit ever more sophisticated methods of outwitting them. The result may be a return to exam-based assessment with rigorous body searches and surveillance in the exam room to detect illicit recording devices. Both scenarios are unpleasant distractions from the purpose of education. The curriculum and its forms of assessment will continue to be shaped by fears of plagiarism in other less negative ways, however. Assessments will become more innovative, as tutors cannot repeat tired essay questions year after year. Instead, the essay may be partially replaced by more creative activities, more analytical comparisons between unlikely texts or exercises that include a component of information gathering in which websites and critical texts may be sourced and assessed. The texts under study may become less canonical. It is harder to find a website offering essays on John Ford's *Perkin Warbeck* (1634) than those selling Shakespeare's *King Lear* (1605). Adapting to these varied forms of assessment will develop your skills of analysis and research methods, while studying marginalised texts will broaden your knowledge and enhance your understanding of canon formation. It is clear that the impact of plagiarism upon the subject of Literature and the canon itself must not be underestimated. What is surprising is that the question of originality, in a discipline that prizes originality, is not the focus of more open, rigorous and intellectual debate at the heart of every literature student's first year.

2.6 How to read: ways of avoiding plagiarism

The first way to avoid plagiarism is to have a clear understanding of what constitutes it. Even when you refer to an author, text or website, if you haven't employed exact quotations and precise referencing, then you could still be accused of plagiarism. Acknowledging an author in your bibliography, or putting quotation marks around some but not all of an extract still constitutes plagiarism. Your department's website or handbook will tell you which referencing system to use, but the main rule of all systems is to be consistent: use the same style for every reference in an essay. Stylebooks on presentation are often complex and off-putting tomes (the sixth edition of the MLA handbook runs to 360 pages) but familiarity with the basic requirements is necessary to prevent accusations of fraud. I have given a guide to the most widely used system, the MLA, in chapter 6: References, complete with examples of how to incorporate quotations, summaries and references into your essays. Here are some more tips:

- In order to reference the sources of your argument correctly, you will need to be clear when making notes which are your own words and which the thoughts of other people. There are some simple practical steps you can take to distinguish the two: if writing, use a different coloured pen for your own words and those of the critic; if typing, use a different font, embolden or italicise one of the two. If you establish a simple system from the start, such as always italicising your own notes that accompany words copied from primary sources, then the chances of sticking to your system, understanding your notes and not accidentally plagiarising are high. You must also distinguish between verbatim records of critics and summaries of their work. I'd also like to sound a note of caution about lecture notes. Lecturers can be guilty of plagiarism, too. You should always distinguish between their words and your own, not least therefore in case their words are not their own, and another marker may recognise, or undertake a search for them.
- Use reliable, recommended sources. Don't rely on websites of notes for your primary quotations: quotations and poems may not be accurately reproduced. You should always check against a text, or a reliable full-text website, such as Bartleby.com (http://www.bartleby.com). Many of the websites offering literature study guides are plagiarised themselves, as well as being badly written, inaccurate and below the standard expected of undergraduate work. It is worth remembering that anyone can publish their work by launching their own web-pages. Reputable websites and printed texts have undergone the scrutiny of editors and peers through several drafts before they are published. I have included a selection of reputable sites written by experts at the end of this chapter; your tutor may be able to suggest some more for particular topics.
- The most valuable resource for avoiding plagiarism is time. If you allow time to research, to draft, edit and rewrite your essays you are less likely to

make mistakes in referencing – or failing to reference – material, nor will you be tempted to plagiarise simply because you have five assignments due and only a week to write them in. When reading texts in the first place, you should also observe some rituals. You should read in silence with a pen in your hand, a dictionary to hand and perhaps at a table. If you are surrounded by noise and distractions you are unlikely to be concentrating fully, which can easily lead to errors in note-taking. Furthermore, reading at a desk, perhaps in a library, is a clear way to make the necessary distinction discussed at the beginning of this chapter between reading as leisure and reading for study. It is a way to take yourself seriously as a critic and to regard the business of analysing texts as a professional activity.

2.7 What to read

One of the many unfortunate consequences of plagiarism's high profile and the draconian punishment meted out to perpetrators is that some students become afraid of committing it inadvertently and so stop reading what are known as 'secondary texts' altogether. The idea of 'primary' and 'secondary' texts will already be familiar to you but to recap, primary texts are usually the editions of the novels, plays and poems that you will focus on for a module. You might expect them to be literary and canonical and to have coherence as a group (all from one period, genre or literary movement, all by one author, or all by a group of authors deemed to have connections, for example, of ethnic or religious background). As we have seen, increasingly, however, curricula have expanded to include the work of marginalised and contemporary authors, biographical writings, public documents, religious tracts and other works of non-fiction alongside well-known literary texts. Secondary texts are usually examples of the critical approaches outlined in 2.4, read to facilitate our interpretation of the 'primary' text. Through a presentation of extrinsic factors (such as historical context) or examination of intrinsic features (stylistic, for example), secondary texts assist our understanding of what the literary text is 'about'. We read them for information. We don't read them as creative works themselves, and rarely in order to appreciate their style. We rarely study them for their own sake outside courses on Critical Theory.

Because of the hierarchy of the reading list, it is easy to understand the primary text to be the main subject of study with secondary texts, as tools for interpretation, as optional. Both the student who fears inadvertent plagiarism, and the student who fears the destruction of the books that she or he loves, regard the secondary text with trepidation. This terminology of primary and

Here is a reading list from a course on Tragedy

Primary texts

Chekhov, Anton. *Three Sisters*. 1897. Trans. Michael Frayn. London: Methuen, 2003.

Euripides. *Medea and Other Plays*. Trans. Philip Vellacott. London: Penguin, 1963.

Kane, Sarah. *Phaedra's Love*. 2000. London: Methuen, 2002.

Shakespeare, William. *Titus Andronicus*. Ed. Jonathan Bate. London: Thomas Nelson, 1995.

Shakespeare, William. *Romeo and Juliet*. c. 1598. Ed. Jill L. Levenson. Oxford: Oxford University Press, 2000.

Sophocles. *Three Theban Plays*. Trans. Robert Fagels. London: Penguin, 1984.

Indicative secondary texts

Aristotle. *Poetics*. Trans. Malcolm Heath. London: Penguin, 1996.

Artaud, Antonin. *The Theatre and Its Double*. Trans. Victor Corti. London: Calder, 1970.

Benjamin, Walter. *The Origin of German Tragic Drama*. Trans. John Osborne. London: Verso, 2002.

Eagleton, Terry. *Sweet Violence: The Idea of the Tragic*. Oxford: Blackwell, 2003.

Dollimore, Jonathan. *Radical Tragedy*. 2nd ed. New York: Harvester Wheatsheaf, 1989.

Loraux, Nicole. *Tragic Ways of Killing a Woman*. Cambridge, MA: Harvard University Press, 1987.

Nietzsche, Friedrich. *The Birth of Tragedy*. Trans. Douglas Smith. Oxford: Oxford University Press, 2000.

Simon, Bennett. *Tragic Drama and the Family: Psychoanalytic Studies from Aeschylus to Beckett*. New Haven: Yale University Press, 1988.

Rabinowitz, Nancy Sorkin. *Anxiety Veiled: Euripides and the Traffic in Women*. Cornell: Cornell University Press, 1993.

Steiner, George. *The Death of Tragedy*. London: Faber, 1995.

Williams, Raymond. *Modern Tragedy*. London: Hogarth, 1992.

secondary reflects and reinforces a culturally established hierarchy; primary and secondary are often considered the direct correlations of 'literature' and 'criticism' where literature is venerated but the meaning of criticism that remains paramount is that of 'finding fault'.

The hierarchy that elevates creativity as a distinct and separate writing practice from criticism has long been debated in literary studies. But accepting this perspective unthinkingly can cause you problems. It can prevent you from reading widely. The danger of study based on the reverence of creative writing and its authors is that it can lead to the reading of literature as biography, the search for an already determined notion of the author in the work, or the attempt to uncover what the author, as the privileged source of the text, intended in her or his work. This is a reductive practice for it treats texts only as sources of information and not as provocations to thought that are part of a wider dialogue. Trying to work out what an author 'means' by a work has been discredited as a critical practice, not least because it reduces literary study to a series of speculations, and reduces poems, novels and plays to codified messages or morals. In an essay called 'The Intentional Fallacy' (1954), New Critics W. K. Wimsatt (1907–75) and Monroe Beardsley (1915–85) argued that an author's intention is anyway unknowable; do authors even fully comprehend what they intend when they begin to write? Furthermore, intentionality as an approach suggests that literary texts do emerge fully formed from the mind of one individual, unshaped or touched by other works, ideas and people. This belief has been challenged by the notion of intertextuality, which recognises instead that texts (and their authors) do not exist in isolation.

Intertextuality The term was coined by the critic Julia Kristeva (1941–) in her influential 1969 essay on the theories of critic Mikhail Bakhtin: dialogism and carnivalism. Kristeva argues that 'any text is constructed as a mosaic of quotations; any text is the absorption and transformation of another' (Moi 37). By this she posited a much wider meaning than the deliberate quotation or imitation of texts (such as Eliot's pastiche of Andrew Marvell's 'To His Coy Mistress' in *The Waste Land*), and the cognisant influence of predecessors (both of which could be construed as a kind of intentionality). She also meant that texts are shaped less consciously by an intricate network of outside forces that are hard (if not impossible) to trace, such as the adoption or rejection of literary conventions, and for this reason an author should never be regarded as a text's sole source. For further reading, Graham Allen's book provides a good introduction to the varieties of literary intertextuality while Mary Orr's comprehensive account focuses on the debate's key thinkers: Kristeva, Roland Barthes (1915–80), Bloom and Gérard Genette (1930–).

So, how should you, as a first-year student, begin to approach the bewildering array of literary theories, methodologies, critical and creative texts? How can you start to make the transition from a school to a university student, or from someone in a claustrophobic love relationship with a text to someone who has achieved a distancing awareness of it? How can you learn to maintain your own voice while satisfying the demands of the discipline? Firstly, you can begin by reconsidering your relationship to primary and secondary, creative and critical works: regard them all equally as texts that are to be questioned. Secondly, expand your definition of the word 'text' from a printed copy of a novel, play or poem to include these and all recorded utterances; critical developments within the discipline as well as our everyday understanding suggest that all cultural artefacts and events are open to reading, to interpretation. Thirdly, familiarising yourself with the idea of intertextuality will help. Consider that all these texts – from adverts to operas – stand in rhetorical relation to each other and within contexts, historical, social and political. Think of these texts as a dynamic of dialogue with each other, constantly renewing and debating ideas, generating new forms. Consider that the process of becoming an undergraduate is the process of finding a position in this world, where you do have a voice not to simply admire a text but to interrogate why, to ask it questions. You can begin to summarise and articulate the theories of critical texts, then test them upon other creative texts. Not only will your reading of creative texts be enriched but you will be able to challenge critical and creative texts alike and in the process become part of the ongoing dialogue, part of 'the endless open exchange' that keeps books alive, that we opened this chapter with. How to do this, how to ask questions, formulate arguments and challenge texts is the subject of the next chapter.

Alternative modes of critical–creative writing

In some institutions you might find that you are explicitly encouraged to abolish distinctions between critical and creative writings in the kinds of assignments and writing activities you are set. Instead of writing essays you might be asked to undertake some sort of 'textual intervention': for example, the **adaptation** of a text from one genre to another that will lead to an understanding of the genres' formal properties and how they influence and create meaning; or an **imitation** in which you come to understand an author's specific style through practice rather than analysis; or the writing of an article with **hypertext** links that enable you to follow a more digressive rather than linear approach to your analyses. The **logbook** that I asked you to keep in chapter 1 might form the basis of a more formal course journal that you are asked to submit to show how your interpretations developed as the course progressed. You may present a portfolio of such activities, sometimes known as a **patchwork text**, that demonstrates a variety of critical–creative writings.

Across the globe, teachers and critics are developing inspired writing practices to assist your learning and to break down the hierarchical approach to studying texts; among them in the UK are Rob Pope and Ben Knights and in the US Robert Scholes and Jerome McGann (I have listed some of their books in the Works Cited below).

2.8 Some recommended websites

This is a selection of recommended online resources about texts, authors and critical issues rather than sites that are primarily text archives or library catalogues. Your university library will also subscribe to all the major literary journals, which can be accessed through its web-pages.

- http://www.litencyc.com – **The Literary Encyclopedia**'s profiles of authors, texts and topics are written by scholars. Their entries, which are growing in number, contain full and up-to-date accounts of critical debates around each author and subject. The site also hosts a useful style guide.
- http://www.contemporarywriters.com – **Contemporary Writers.com** is a British Council initiative. It offers biographies, bibliographies and critical reviews of living UK and Commonwealth writers. It is not primarily aimed at undergraduates but offers accurate and current information that could form a strong starting point for research upon contemporary authors.

Subject gateways

- http://www.intute.ac.uk/artsandhumanities/ – the Universities of Oxford, Manchester Metropolitan and of the Arts London host this hub. It gives access to online humanities resources and tutorials for those in higher and further education as well as the general public, clearly listed under subject headings.
- http://andromeda.rutgers.edu/~jlynch/Lit – **Literary Resources on the Net** is a gateway to sites on English and American literature designed for those in higher education. These sites are accessed through the home-page lists of periods and genres and a search engine.
- http://vos.ucsb.edu – **Voice of the Shuttle** is a famously comprehensive database for the humanities with links to literature, literary theory and gender and sexuality sites among many, many others. The categories on the home page include one of 'unvetted submissions' so that users can determine which resources have been validated through review.

Works cited

Allen, Graham. *Intertextuality*. London: Routledge, 2000.
Anderson, Benedict. *Imagined Communities: Reflections on the Origin and Spread of Nationalism*. London: Verso, 1983.
Andrews, Richard and Sally Mitchell. *Essays in Argument*. London: Middlesex University Press, 2001.
Bhabha, Homi, ed. *Nations and Narration*. London and New York: Routledge, 1990.
Barry, Peter. *Beginning Theory: An Introduction to Literary and Cultural Theory*. 2nd ed. London: Prentice Hall, 1999.

Bloom, Harold. *The Western Canon: The Books and School of the Ages.* 1994. London: Macmillan, 1995.

Briggs, Julia. *Reading Virginia Woolf.* Edinburgh: Edinburgh University Press, 2006.

Butler, Judith. *Bodies that Matter: On the Discursive Limits of 'Sex'.* New York and London: Routledge, 1993.

Butler, Judith. *Excitable Speech: A Politics of the Performative.* New York and London: Routledge, 1997.

Butler, Judith. *Gender Trouble: Feminism and the Subversion of Identity.* New York and London: Routledge, 1990.

Castle, Gregory. *The Blackwell Guide to Literary Theory.* Oxford: Blackwell, 2007.

Culler, Jonathan. *Literary Theory: A Very Short Introduction.* Oxford: Oxford University Press, 1997.

Derrida, Jacques. *Of Grammatology.* Trans. Gayatri Chakravorty Spivak. Baltimore: Johns Hopkins University Press, 1976.

Eagleton, Terry. *Literary Theory: An Introduction.* Oxford: Blackwell, 1983.

Eliot, T. S. 'Tradition and the Individual Talent.' 1919. *Selected Essays.* London: Faber and Faber, 1951. 13–22.

Fish, Stanley. *Is There a Text in this Class? The Authority of Interpretive Communities.* Cambridge, MA: Harvard University Press, 1980.

Foucault, Michel. *The History of Sexuality I: An Introduction.* Trans. Robert Hurley. London: Allen Lane, 1979.

Freud, Sigmund. *The Penguin Freud Library.* 15 vols. Harmondsworth: Penguin, 1974–86.

Gates, Henry Louis. *The Signifying Monkey: A Theory of Afro-American Literary Criticism.* New York: Oxford University Press, 1988.

Gallagher, Catherine and Stephen Greenblatt. *Practicing New Historicism.* Chicago: Chicago University Press, 2000.

Gibaldi, Joseph. *MLA Handbook for Writers of Research Papers.* 6th ed. New York: The Modern Language Association of America, 2003.

Greenblatt, Stephen. *Renaissance Self-Fashioning: From More to Shakespeare.* Chicago: Chicago University Press, 1980.

Harland, Richard. *Literary Theory From Plato to Barthes: An Introductory History.* Houndmills, Basingstoke: Macmillan, 1999.

Hawkes, Terence. *Structuralism and Semiotics.* London: Methuen, 1977.

hooks, bell. *Ain't I a Woman?: Black Women and Feminism.* Boston: South End Press, 1981.

Iser, Wolfgang. *The Implied Reader: Patterns of Communication in Prose Fiction from Bunyan to Beckett.* Baltimore: Johns Hopkins University Press, 1974.

Knights, Ben and Chris Thurgar-Dawson. *Active Reading: Transformative Writing in Literary Studies.* London: Continuum, 2006.

Kristeva, Julia. 'Word, Dialogue and Novel.' 1969. *The Kristeva Reader.* Ed. Toril Moi. Oxford: Blackwell, 1986. 34–61.

Leavis, F. R. *English Literature in Our Time and the University.* London: Chatto & Windus, 1969.

Leavis, F. R. *The Great Tradition: George Eliot, Henry James, Joseph Conrad.* London: Chatto & Windus, 1948.

Leavis, Q. D. *Fiction and the Reading Public.* 1932. London: Chatto & Windus, 1978.

McGann, Jerome. *Radiant Textuality: Literature After the World Wide Web.* New York: Palgrave, 2001.

Murfin, Ross C., ed. *Joseph Conrad: Heart of Darkness.* Case Studies in Contemporary Criticism. 2nd ed. Boston and New York: Bedford / St Martins, 1996.

Norris, Christopher. *Deconstruction: Theory and Practice.* London: Methuen, 1982.

Orr, Mary. *Intertextuality: Debates and Contexts.* Cambridge: Polity, 2003.

Pope, Rob. *The English Studies Book.* 2nd ed. London and New York: Routledge, 2002.

Pope, Rob. *Textual Intervention: Critical and Creative Strategies for Literary Studies.* London: Routledge, 1994.

Robbins, Ruth. *Literary Feminisms.* Transitions. Houndmills: Macmillan Press, 2000.

Rose, Jacqueline. *The Haunting of Sylvia Plath.* London: Virago, 1991.

Royle, Nicholas. *Jacques Derrida.* Routledge Critical Thinkers. London: Routledge, 2003.

Said, Edward. *Orientalism.* London: Penguin, 1985.

Saussure, Ferdinand de. *Course in General Linguistics.* 1916. Trans. Wade Baskin. Intro. Jonathan Culler. London: Fontana Collins, 1974.

Scholes, Robert. *Protocols of Reading.* New Haven and London: Yale University Press, 1991.

Scholes, Robert. *Textual Power: Literary Theory and the Teaching of English.* New Haven and London: Yale University Press, 1985.

Sedgwick, Eve Kosofsky. *Between Men: English Literature and Male Homosocial Desire.* New York: Columbia University Press, 1985.

Smith, Ali. *The Reader.* London: Constable, 2006.

Smith, Barbara. *Toward a Black Feminist Criticism.* 1977. http://webs.wofford.edu/hitchmoughsa/Toward.html

Spivak, Gayatri Chakravorty. *The Post-Colonial Critic: Interviews, Strategies, Dialogues.* Ed. Sarah Harasym. New York and London: Routledge, 1990.

Todorov, Tzvetan. *Introduction to Poetics.* Trans. Richard Howard. Brighton: The Harvester Press, 1981.

Veeser, H. Aram, ed. *The New Historicism.* London and New York: Routledge, 1989.

Wimsatt, W. K. *The Verbal Icon: Studies in the Meaning of Poetry, and Two Preliminary Essays Written in Collaboration with Monroe C. Beardsley.* 1954. London: Methuen, 1970.

Woolf, Virginia. 'Character in Fiction.' *The Essays of Virginia Woolf.* Ed. Andrew McNeillie. Vol. 3. London: Hogarth Press, 1988. 420–38.

Chapter 3

Argument

3.1 Having something to say

Sometimes students become so preoccupied with the format of essays – writing an introduction and a conclusion – that they forget the essay's main purpose: it must have something to say on a particular subject. And ironically, the more you struggle with essays, the more likely you are to be directed away from the topic and the discipline of Literature towards a non-subject-specific guidebook or to generic study-skills classes where formulae for writing good essays are demonstrated. But however well-versed you become in the structure of essays – introduction, middle, conclusion, bibliography – unless you actually have something to say, your essay will never succeed. Readers might forgive an abrupt ending or a referencing error if you offer some interesting perspectives; focusing instead on the format and conventions of essays, in diverting your attention away from their content, can be positively detrimental. Since the French Renaissance scholar Michel de Montaigne (1533–92) entitled his 1580 book *Essais*, the term 'essay' has come to denote a polished composition on a topic, losing an earlier meaning that is very helpful to writers. Originally an essay was not a finished treatise but an attempt or an endeavour (an assay). Returning to this meaning, with its emphasis upon the discussion of a subject rather than a masterful verdict upon it, should help alleviate some of the anxiety experienced when approaching an essay. In other words, you should spend more time thinking about the points you'd like to make than upon shoehorning them into a neat conclusion or upon composing a definitive answer to the question. But, of course, the process of finding something to say should begin not when you face an essay question, but when you start reading.

As we have seen in the last chapter, simply expressing admiration or disdain for a text won't suffice for something to say. Instead of just a personal value judgement your essay must offer one or more propositions; you are being asked to persuade your reader of a theory or viewpoint. You are not being asked to describe texts or simply show what you have read; you are being asked to form an *argument* about a text or texts. In everyday usage, argument, like 'criticism', is a word that has negative connotations. It is used to describe an event in which two or more people vehemently disagree with one another, often losing their tempers in the process; each person convinced that she or he is in the right, increasingly unwilling to concede ground. In this sense an argument is usually, although not always, enacted verbally rather than on paper or in print. It is always associated with disagreement, high emotion and often with a loss of reasoning; none of which are qualities you can imagine being able to reproduce on demand or be rewarded for in the course of your academic study.

Response

Why do people argue?
List as many *functions* of arguments as you can. We are not hoping to register all the possible causes of disputes in this activity but trying to consider the purposes different arguments are intended to serve. For example, a young woman might have a row with her mother about wanting to have a tattoo. The cause of disagreement might be that the mother finds tattoos unattractive or doesn't want her daughter to do something irrevocable that she might later regret. But for the daughter, the unarticulated function of the argument is to assert her sense of identity and independence from her parent.

Example of argument	Its function
1 A young woman wants a tattoo and argues with her mother who forbids her from getting one.	to assert independence
2	
3	
4	
5	

Can any of these functions be related to those an essay or seminar discussion might serve?

There are qualities of this everyday understanding of argument that can be usefully retained and developed as a mainstay of academic literary study. The first is that arguments are dialogic: more than one voice is heard in an argument; you cannot argue with yourself. The second follows on from this and is an adjustment to the conception of disagreement as negative: instead of associating argument with acts of personal hostility between individuals, reconsider it as an exchange of ideas, a dialogue. This is important. On a larger, societal scale, argument is the manifestation of democracy; dissent is the enactment of difference. We do not all think alike. It is the purpose of this chapter to introduce these positive definitions of argument; the words like 'dialogue' and 'rhetoric' that are associated with it; to consider argument in relation to stories and other communicative acts; and to demonstrate ways of writing arguments, of generating dialogues with texts, of finding something to say.

3.2 Rethinking dialogue: Mikhail Mikhailovich Bakhtin (1895–1975)

Despite the fact that in his lifetime only two books were published under his name, and that only fragments of these were translated into English before the 1980s, the theories of the Russian critic Mikhail Bakhtin and those with whom he worked (the poet and musicologist Valerian Nicolaevich Voloshinov (1894/5–1936) and the critic Pavel Nikolaevich Medvedev (1891–1938)) have profoundly influenced many areas of twentieth-century thought. There are two words that have become primarily associated with the Bakhtin circle (as they are collectively known): dialogue and carnival. *The Problems of Dostoevsky's Poetics* (published in 1929 but completed earlier that decade) and *Rabelais and His World* (a thesis completed in 1940 but only published in 1965), as their titles suggest, are ostensibly concerned with literature, but in them Bakhtin outlined the very nature of human consciousness and as such their impact has been felt in the fields of psychology, philosophy, sociology, anthropology and education, as well as linguistics and literary criticism. His books were optimistic examinations of the possibility of intellectual and spiritual freedom, which accounts for their immediate popularity in the circumscribed environment of the Soviet Union in both the late 1920s and the 1960s. His consideration of the structures and forces opposing such freedoms may also be another reason for the paucity of his published output; in 1929 he was arrested and sentenced to five years in a concentration camp (then exiled to Kazakhstan when ill health made this untenable), it is thought for reasons associated with his Russian Orthodox Christian faith. Since then the works of the Bakhtin circle have been celebrated by those on both the left and the right of the political spectrum. His investment in the freedom to express dissent and engage in dialogue is clear to all.

What unites all the writings of Bakhtin, Voloshinov and Medvedev is their ceaseless concern with the nature of discourse (a sequence or body of communication understood and employed by particular groups, usually unconsciously). They believed that every discourse, written or spoken, is an expression of ideology, that is, it expresses a view of the world, inevitably coloured by your social group or standing. Voloshinov and Medvedev sought in their earlier work to examine discourse in relation to context and not as an abstract system of signs like linguists inspired by Ferdinand de Saussure had done. Indeed, their critiques of Russian formalism were founded in the Marxist notion of historical materialism, stressing the importance of history and the situation in which every communicative act occurs. Bakhtin's work clearly exemplifies these socio-critical dimensions; for instance, *Rabelais and His World* is a study not just of the writer but also of the popular festivals of his period. In it Bakhtin celebrated the 'carnival consciousness' of the medieval world, in which parody and play undermined the static conservative view of official society. For Bakhtin, the genre of the novel is the prime example of 'carnivalised' literature, because, like the medieval carnival, it is a site where orthodoxies are contested, satirised and undermined; its varied voices – of narrator and characters – allow for dialogue. Although the publication of this second work and the idea of the carnivalesque aroused considerable excitement for both the initial Russian- and then English-speaking audiences, it typifies and reiterates the dominant theories and practices of the Bakhtin circle; it is concerned with debate and dialogue.

It is Bakhtin's notion of dialogue that is particularly germane to our concerns in this book. As literary critics, we can examine novels for many-languagedness as he did (he used the term heteroglossia to denote the multiple languages of various social groups that a novel must be composed of), but it is his theory of how being and meaning are created that may help us begin the process of having a dialogue with literary texts, of finding something to say. For Bakhtin, being is always a process, a process that necessitates constant dialogue with the world. Without interaction it is impossible for an individual to have a sense of self: I cannot see my 'spatial and temporal limits (my bodily extremities and my birth/death respectively)' (Morris 247) and so I depend upon the perception of others to achieve an idea of myself and, vice versa, they rely upon me to gain a picture of themselves. Bakhtin argues that being and meaning are continually redefined, through a lifetime's dialogue with others. (It should be noted that this is not often a conscious process.) Furthermore, for Bakhtin every utterance is not only a response to a previous utterance but anticipates a future response. It is in this sense that we should consider our roles as readers when we approach a literary or critical text, as essential contributors to the endless process of meaning-making, as was suggested by Smith, Woolf and Todorov at the beginning of chapter 2: Reading. In analysing texts we are not somehow damaging or diminishing them but producing their meanings because they cannot exist in isolation, just as we are defined in relation to others (for example, I recognise my Britishness most distinctly when I am abroad or my small stature when I am in the company of the statuesque). What distinguishes reading inside the academy (at university) from reading outside it, as we have seen in the last chapter, is that as literary critics we are trying to make the process of meaning-making explicit. In terms of identity (being), we stop taking part in the process of self-definition when we die – although we will continue to be redefined by those who remember us – but the process of making a text's meaning is one that will never end.

Response

This endless process of meaning-making is evident in the history of literary criticism. There are several series of literary studies that examine the different interpretations of individual texts since production; for example, the Palgrave Series edited by Nicolas Tredell includes analyses of the reception of texts as historically diverse as Chaucer's General Prologue to *The Canterbury Tales* and Toni Morrison's *Beloved*. This is an activity that you can undertake yourself; you should consult your subject librarian to assist you in your search for articles, reviews and monographs on your chosen text.

Select a text that you are currently studying and either (a) find a book of collected criticism upon it or (b) aim to compile a history of its criticism yourself. What themes can you detect? Would the changing reputation or reception of a text form the basis of an interesting essay or seminar discussion?

The word 'dialogue' has clear democratic connotations incorporating the free and continual exchange of ideas among those who are equal in power; for Bakhtin, monologue, its opposite, describes the discourses of ruling classes and authoritarian regimes that claim that there is only one view of the world. As literary critics, we can analyse the dialogic nature of novels and consider whether poetry tends towards monologism in the singular voicedness of its form, as he thought, but it is perhaps Bakhtin's urging of the democratic principle of dialogue that is most valuable in our approach to the subject of reading texts as a whole. It is our democratic right and responsibility to find something to say to them, to give them meaning, and to let them give it to us, too.

3.3 Stories, arguments and democracy

What does it mean to say that arguments are the manifestation of democracy? The state of democracy – and the democratic State in which everyone has equal rights – is dependent upon the free expression of opinion. People are allowed to think differently from one another, and from those who have been

Further reading

For introductions to Bakhtin's writings see Simon Dentith's *Bakhtinian Thought*, Pam Morris's *Bakhtin Reader*, and Sue Vice's *Introducing Bakhtin*. Tzvetan Todorov provides an accessible overview and reading of the principle theories of the Bakhtin circle in *Mikhail Bakhtin: The Dialogical Principle*; Wayne Booth examines the relationship between form and content in his introduction to Bakhtin's *The Problems of Dostoevsky's Poetics*; an example of the influence of Bakhtin on literary criticism can be found in David Lodge's collection of essays, *After Bakhtin*. Bakhtin's key texts are also listed in the Works Cited at the end of this chapter.

granted powers of government. In a non-democratic State, subjects (those who are not in power) are instructed what to think and any expression of difference or dissent is forbidden, as was Bakhtin's experience in Russia in the 1920s. An argument is a democratic, or dialogic, mode of interaction by definition; it is constituted of differing views: as we've already seen one person in isolation cannot have an argument, nor is the communication of concord between several people an argument. In an argument a position is presented and then recipients offer alternative viewpoints. It is also a continuous process; one utterance follows another, progressing or perhaps regressing by return to previously made points, through a period of time. Non-argument, or mono-logic, modes of interaction do not rely upon a challenge for their meaning to be created. For example, a university lecture is a form of communication in which information is passed from the lecturer to the passive audience of students. The lecture is considered complete and over without a formal space for audience discussion once the hour is up and the lecturer leaves the room. A literature seminar may (and should) allow for the lecture to be transformed into a form of argument when its ideas are debated and challenged. In the first, non-argument scenario, meaning is created by one person (the lecturer); in an ideal version of the second, argument-based form, the seminar, meaning(s) are constructed and developed by many (the students). This does not mean that the seminar will degenerate into chaotic dispute – although conversation might be heated – rather, that the understanding of the studied texts will be negotiated, developed and tested by members of the group and not simply stated by the lecturer. One of the challenges for new students is to perceive that the literature lecture is not a monologue but the beginning, or part, of a dialogue.

In the school curricula designed by the Conservative governments of the 1980s (see chapter 2: Reading) in which the teaching of literary classics was part of a process encouraging English nationalism, literature itself was tacitly understood to be a non-argument form. School pupils were expected to read the tales of heroism and national victory and unquestioningly receive their meaning as a message about positive English virtues. The pupils' written assignments, taking the form of practical criticism, did not examine, let alone question, the ideology of the tales but simply 'discovered' why they were valued texts through the structured analysis of form; or, through the vaguer methodology of character studies, they were encouraged to sympathise with the heroic protagonists (and thus identify with their patriotism). We have already seen that the movement from practical criticism to cultural studies, in the discipline of English, challenges this opposition in which stories appear to be the opposite of arguments. The more recent critical schools examine the persuasive powers of every text and attempt to uncover its ideology. In the last chapter I mentioned that some students feel coerced by such critical approaches. This is an implicit recognition that literary criticism is an argument form of communication: the students impulsively want to argue with it. The most important step that you can take as a first-year student of English is to recognise that stories also employ persuasive techniques and that you should stand at as much of a critical distance from them as you might impulsively from works of criticism. Critical and literary texts are just different genres of narrative.

3.4 The folded paper: how to stand at a distance and start a dialogue with a text

This reading practice, shown on the opposite page, was devised by S. L. Meyer: it asks you to speak for and against the text you are studying and physically reconstructs the idea of a dialogue (reproduced in Andrews and Mitchell 156). It encourages you to use your own voice to question the text because sometimes writing an essay in an 'appropriate' academic style can divert your attention from the topic and your ideas.

3.4.1 Example of a folded-paper dialogue with a literary text

Edith Wharton's 1928 novel *The Children* is set in the milieu of wealthy Americans travelling in Europe. Martin Boyne, the middle-aged protagonist, encounters a family of unsupervised children (the Wheaters) on a cruise to Venice and although he is on the way to meet Rose Sellars, a widow to whom he is expecting to become engaged, he develops an infatuation with Judith Wheater, who at fifteen is the eldest sibling and a mother figure to the other children. The Wheater family are the biological and step-children of a 'big red-

Fold a piece of paper in half vertically (or create a Word document with two columns, if you are working on a computer). On the left side of the page you will make statements about what the text is saying and on the right side you'll question these statements. You can subject any text to this process but the size of the original will determine how far you break it down. You might attempt to collapse a sonnet into an analysis of every line, a short essay into every paragraph, but a novel may be considered in larger chunks or you might examine only the major monologues of a play. (You are perhaps less likely to misrepresent a text if you consider smaller components or significant passages and build up your overall argument from them rather than attempt to summarise the argument of, say, a whole novel and then question it in its entirety.) Your left-side summaries should be succinct and declarative while your right-hand questions should be tentative and as numerous as you can manage. Your questions may lead in several different directions and explore a variety of issues; nevertheless, upon completion of the task you may find a consistent strain of argument that could form the basis of an essay or seminar debate. In this activity you are encouraged to seek out the text's contradictions, ambiguities and omissions but upon completion you will also have a sense of the sequence and construction of the text's argument.

faced Chicagoan who was at Harvard with him [Boyne] and who has since become one of the showiest of New York millionaires' (Wharton 5). Cliffe Wheater's newly earned, rather than inherited, wealth is an emblem of his modernity, as are the enormous complexities of his family and marital history: married thrice, the second time to the exotically monikered Zinnia Lacrosse, a film star, he has casually adopted the offspring of his first wife's second husband, Prince Buondelmonte, remarrying the first Mrs Wheater when this 'wicked' European prince was discovered to be a bigamist. Rose Sellars, meanwhile, embodies propriety and 'old' money. In the prehistory of the novel, Boyne wooed Sellars during her unhappy marriage, but she remained faithful to her husband, despite her attraction to Boyne. Their courtship through letters is continued throughout the duration of the novel; in her astute readings, Sellars is aware of Boyne's desire for the 'little girl–mother' right from the start, and long before he admits it. Some critics of *The Children* have chosen to read the novel as an allegory in this way: Boyne has to choose between the ways of old respectable New York, Rose Sellars, and the freedoms of the new society, Judith. But I can't help feeling that this focus on Wharton's well-worn theme is a distraction from the novel's explicit focus on the taboo of an unsuitable attraction, of paedophiliac desire.

Here are the first three paragraphs of chapter 23. Judith has come increasingly to rely upon Boyne as an ally against the follies of her parents. In order to escape from being split as a family unit and returned to the guardianship of their biological parents, Judith and the children have run away to Switzerland to be near Boyne and Mrs Sellars. Boyne is reflecting upon the situation and his feelings for Mrs Sellars:

> It was growing more and more evident to Boyne that he could recover his old vision of Mrs Sellars only when they were apart. He began to think this must be due to his having loved her so long from a distance, having somehow, in consequence of their separation, established with her an ideal relation to which her slightest misapprehension, her least failure to say just what he expected, was a recurring menace.
>
> At first the surprise of finding her, after his long absence, so much younger and more vivid than his remembrance, the glow of long-imagined caresses, the whole enchanting harmony of her presence, had hushed the inner discord. But though she was dearer to him than ever, all free communication seemed to have ceased between them – he could regain it only during those imaginary conversations in which it was he who sustained both sides of the dialogue.
>
> This was what happened when he had walked off the pain and bewilderment of their last talk. For two hours he tramped the heights, unhappy, confused, struggling between the sense of her unreasonableness and of his own predicament; then gradually there stole back on him the serenity always associated with the silent sessions of his thought and hers. On what seemed to him the fundamental issues – questions of fairness, kindness, human charity in the widest meaning – when had she ever failed him in these wordless talks? His position with regard to the Wheater children (hadn't he admitted it to her?) was unreasonable, indefensible, was whatever else she chose to call it; yes, but it was also human, and that would touch her in the end. He had no doubt that when they met the next day she would have her little solution ready, and be prepared to smile with him over their needless perturbation.   (Wharton 237–8).

My example of the folded-paper dialogue is shown on the opposite page.

The two things that are immediately striking from this activity are that the story is narrated from one point of view (Boyne's) and it feels quite restricted in this sense. In asking questions, I was constantly trying to imagine what Mrs Sellars really thinks and not just what Boyne imagines. I also became slightly suspicious of Boyne and the fact that there is a gap between his narration and the story being told. He is what is known as an 'unreliable narrator' because we suspect that he is twisting the truth to suit himself and if we were to hear another narrator's account, it would tell a different story. This kind of narrator is often deployed when there are issues of morality at stake;

Statements about what the text is saying	My questions
Paragraph 1	
Boyne was feeling increasingly that he could only love Rose Sellars when they were apart.	Is his relationship with Mrs Sellars built entirely in his mind? Has he always had the wrong impression of her? Or is it that in the past they did agree on matters but now she challenges what he says and he just doesn't like it?
Paragraph 2	
She was much younger than he'd remembered but they found it hard to talk to each other. He could only have imaginary conversations with her.	Has he been comparing her with Judith so he'd remembered her as really old? Is she suspicious of his feelings for Judith and this is making conversation difficult?
Paragraph 3	
When he got away from her he was able to feel calm by resuming the kind of imaginary conversations they had before.	Is he deluding himself by imagining things he'd like her to say? What if she still criticises him because she's concerned about his attachment not just to the children but especially to Judith?
She thought his attachment to the children was unreasonable but he was sure she would soon change her mind.	Surely she is not going to change her mind? Wouldn't we hear something quite different if the story was told from Mrs Sellars's point of view? Does Mrs Sellars represent the view of society? The reader? Edith Wharton?

famous unreliable narrators in literature include Humbert Humbert in Nabokov's *Lolita* (1955), guilty of paedophilia, murderers Patrick Bateman in *American Psycho* (1991) by Brett Easton Ellis, and Frederick Clegg in *The Collector* (1963) by John Fowles. In these examples there is a gap, a dialogue, between the narrator's morality and that of the author. Having determined that Boyne is unreliable, it would now be worth examining the rest of the text for other types of narrative (direct speech, alternative points of view) to see if his assessment of the situation is challenged. Indeed, it would be a rewarding act of creative criticism to rewrite scenes from the novel from Rose Sellars's perspective.

Response

Now try the folded-paper activity on a literary text you are currently studying.

We can see that in folding the paper we are undertaking two activities: the first, on the left-hand side, is an act of comprehension, an attempt to pick out and summarise the key point of each paragraph or section; the second, on the right, is an exploratory challenge to these ideas. It is a tentative challenge because at this stage you are not going to show it to anyone, so you are free to try things out, to experiment. But it's also worth stressing how important the first part of the exercise is. Writing something down is certainly a way to discover whether you have understood what you are reading. As I stressed at the end of chapter 2: Reading, reading as an academic activity often involves writing, so that your reading (your interpretation) can be identified on paper. The folded-paper activity can help you to recognise uncertainties in your reading and ambiguities in a text that can be raised in a seminar or form a point of discussion in an essay. If your starting point was a literary text, the next stage of the process might be to select a critical text to test or answer the questions you raised on the left-hand side of your paper.

3.4.2 Example of a folded-paper dialogue with a critical text in order to prepare a dialogue for an essay or seminar discussion

The writing of Raymond Williams crossed many disciplines including fiction, drama and journalism, but it is for his work as a cultural materialist that he is most widely known; indeed he is credited as one of the originators of Cultural Studies. Williams's work is concerned with charting the relationship between social and intellectual history since the Industrial Revolution. Two of his most important works, *Culture and Society* (1958) and *Keywords: A Vocabulary of Culture and Society* (1976; revised and expanded version 1983), examine the changing meanings of words like 'democracy', 'class', 'art' and 'culture'. His critics find fault with his readings of novels as largely realist forms, refusing to consider symbolic possibilities, for example, and more vociferously, his failure to recognise the significance of gender; when Williams talks of man he usually means man, not humanity. His 1973 book *The Country and the City* analyses the perceived dichotomy between rural and urban life through a survey of texts from the eighteenth to the early-twentieth century with reference to economic and social history.

Here is the beginning of chapter 1: 'Country and City'.

'Country' and 'City' are very powerful words, and this is not surprising when we remember how much they seem to stand for in the experience of human communities. In English, 'country' is both a nation and a part of a 'land'; 'the country' can be the whole society or its rural area. In the long history of human settlements, this connection between the land from which directly or indirectly we all get our living and the achievements of human society has been deeply known. And one of these achievements has been the city: the capital, the large town, a distinctive form of civilisation.

On the actual settlements, which in the real history have been astonishingly varied, powerful feelings have gathered and have been generalised. On the country has gathered the idea of a natural way of life: of peace, innocence and simple virtue. On the city has gathered the idea of an achieved centre: of learning, communication, light. Powerful hostile associations have also developed: on the city as a place of noise, worldliness and ambition; on the country as a place of backwardness, ignorance, limitation. A contrast between country and city, as fundamental ways of life, reaches back into classical times.

Yet the real history, throughout, has been astonishingly varied. The 'country way of life' has included the very different practices of hunters, pastoralists, farmers and factory farmers, and its organisation has varied from the tribe and the manor to the feudal estate, from the small peasantry and tenant farmers to the rural commune, from the *latifundia* [large estates in Latin America] and the plantation to the large capitalist enterprise and the state farm. The city, no less, has been of many kinds: state capital, administrative base, religious centre, market-town, port and mercantile depot, military barracks, industrial concentration. Between the cities of ancient and medieval times and the modern metropolis or conurbation there is a connection of name and in part of function, but nothing like identity. Moreover, in our own world, there is a wide range of settlements between the traditional poles of country and city: suburb, dormitory town, shanty town, industrial estate. Even the idea of the village, which seems simple, shows in actual history a wide variation: as to size and character, and internally in its variation between dispersed and nuclear settlements, in Britain as clearly as anywhere.

In and through these differences, all the same, certain images and associations persist; and it is the purpose of this book to describe and analyse them, to see them in relation to the historically varied experience.   (Williams 1–2)

Response

Try the folded-paper activity on this passage from Williams's introduction.

My response:

Statements about what the text is saying	My questions
Paragraph 1	
Country and city are powerful words. Country can mean a whole nation or just its rural area. There is a connection between the land and the city.	Surely you can argue that this connection is not 'deeply known'? What is the connection? Do we really all 'get our living' from the land?
Paragraph 2	
There are strong and generalised oppositions in the way that the country and the city are viewed. These have existed since classical times.	Is he going to suggest that these oppositions are false? Can I find literary texts and other documents that will support or challenge these notions?
Paragraph 3	
The real history of rural and urban places is not homogenous but is 'astonishingly varied'.	Where does his notion of 'real history' come from? Why have the oppositions been formed then, if available documentation suggests they are false or a simplification?
Paragraph 4	
He is going to analyse the persistent images and associations in this book.	Will this contradict his assertion of difference in the statement above? Is he going to explain why these associations have been formed?

The process of questioning a literary or critical text, like a dialogue, should be ongoing. It might be circular rather than linear: once you have identified a critic's position, you might want to test it on some literary texts, and then return to the critic to test her or his words in the new light of your reading. We can use the terminology of logic (the formal system in philosophy deployed to test the truth of an argument) to categorise these approaches: taking a critical proposition and then finding examples from literary texts to support or refute it is a form of **deductive** reasoning, in which your argument moves from general principles to particular details. The opposite mode of logic, **induction**, starts by looking at specific facts and uses them to build a general principle. For example, if we were to start constructing an argument by using the work of Williams above, having read the introduction we might state, 'Cities in literature are always represented as advanced centres of learning, communication, light but also noise, worldliness and ambition', and then seek to support or refute this by looking for examples in literary texts. This would be an example of deduction. We started with a broad principle and looked for details in literature to back it up or disprove it. Often an essay question is a general proposition that you are being asked to consider and so the research you undertake for it is deductive reasoning. Alternatively, we might start by examining a number of texts to see how rural life is depicted and then use the weight of these examples to write a proposition. We would be starting with specific examples from our notes and using them to compose a general theory and thus employing inductive reasoning. I mentioned earlier that critics reading the corpus of Edith Wharton's fiction, noting the persistent theme of 'new' versus 'old' money, have induced from these examples a general principle roughly along the lines of, 'The preoccupation with "old" and "new" money in Wharton's prose represents, not just American society's anxiety about the erosion of tradition, but also the possible freedoms that a new social order might allow.' I suggested that the flaw with this kind of inductive theory-making is that it can blind the reader to other textual concerns and interpretations.

Response

How do you normally compose an argument? Through inductive or deductive reasoning? What are the advantages and disadvantages of both methods? Where do general principles come from?

The folded-paper responses are informal ways of creating dialogues with texts. You don't need to show them to anyone. They can form the disposable origins of a polished essay, or the notes for a seminar discussion. There is, however, an ancient and formal discipline with methodologies for the creation and presentation of arguments: the discipline of rhetoric.

3.5 What is rhetoric?

What is rhetoric? Commonly defined as the art of using language to influence or persuade people, like 'argument' and 'criticism' the term has been sullied: in everyday speech it is sometimes used to mean a hollow kind of talk employed to persuade people to believe or buy something, or to behave in a way that goes against their better judgement or wishes (by politicians, advertisers or salespeople, for instance). It is perceived as a stylistic manipulation that consciously stands at some distance from the 'truth'. But as we have begun – and will go on – to examine, recent critics consider that every text can be scrutinised for its ideological content and its persuasive appeal, and not just those texts, like adverts, whose explicit purpose is persuasion. It was an automatic assumption for the original Greek rhetoricians of the fifth century BC that all forms of expression sought to persuade; they were interested in the method of that persuasion. The Greeks studied the language of poetry, drama and public speeches for pedagogical reasons, in order to emulate them. Imitating successful speeches was the dominant form of education; it was the way to personal gain and career advancement. For many centuries then, the rhetoric of texts was studied for the purposes of providing a model of how to structure one's own speeches; this is indicated by the fact that in the US the study of rhetoric is known as Composition. But during the last century, the rhetorical appeal of all texts has become the purpose of study in itself: it is the *substance* and not the *means* of study.

3.6 A *very* brief survey of Classical rhetoric

It is impossible to summarise a discipline that has spanned thousands of years in a few hundred words. Instead, my overview draws attention to three things: the origins of rhetoric in democracy; the fluctuating perception of the bond between the integrity of the orator and the 'truth' throughout history; and the relationship between the study of rhetoric and the study of literature. My account also introduces some key figures and terms so that you have a starting point from which to begin further investigations, should you so wish.

3.6.1 The five canons of rhetoric

The origins of rhetoric as a formulated art are attributed to Corax in fifth-century BC Syracuse. His strategies for the organisation of a speech were designed to help ordinary citizens who needed to represent themselves in court. Following the deposition of the despot, Thrasybulus, democracy had been introduced and the citizens of Syracuse were seeking the return of property that had been appropriated under his rule. They had no record or proof of ownership and so relied on their powers of speech and persuasion to win back what was rightfully theirs. Although none of Corax's own writings survive, we know of him through references in the subsequent writings of Plato (427?–347 BC), Aristotle (384–322 BC), Cicero (106–43 BC) and Quintilian (AD 35?–100?). His formula of proem (introduction), narration (the proposition summarised into a statement), arguments (for and against) and peroration (a rousing conclusion) is one that they developed and that has been basically adhered to ever since. It is quite characteristic of the original rhetorical formula to be concretised in a period of political upheaval; the long history of the discipline charts a revival of interest in each period of revolution or social instability. From the start the powers of rhetoric were bound to democracy and citizenship, and necessitated dialogue with an audience.

The total methodology of how to prepare and present an argument verbally, which was developed from Corax's structure for a speech in court, is sometimes known as the five canons of rhetoric. These stages have aroused varying degrees of attention in handbooks through the ages. Their Latin names are **inventio, dispositio, elocutio, memoria** and **pronunciatio**.

Inventio, sounding like invention, is the discovery of arguments. It is what we are concerned with in this chapter – finding something to say – and in contemporary essay-writing guidebooks is often given suprisingly little attention. George Quackenbos, a nineteenth-century American rhetorician who wrote textbooks on Composition, recognised both the importance of this stage and the difficulty that students often have in finding something to say: 'It is [invention] that furnishes the material of composition, and on which, in a great measure, its value depends. Here moreover, lies most of the difficulty which the young experience in writing' (quoted in Corbett and Connors 522). Quackenbos suggested some techniques for students to come up with ideas but because he was teaching composition as a subject in its own right, and not allied to another subject, he also listed hundreds of topics for them to write about, a common practice in the teaching of rhetoric.

Dispositio, the next stage, is the arrangement of material, of the ideas that have been gathered in inventio. Some rhetoricians refined Corax's organisation into five parts – the introduction, the proposition, the arguments for, the case against, the conclusion – while Aristotle offered only two – the proposition and the proof. We will consider the structure of essays in the next chapter, while strenuously agreeing with Quackenbos that this should not even be considered until a process or processes of inventio have been undertaken.

Elocutio refers not to the art of speaking but to style. Style is a word with very positive connotations; we speak admiringly of someone's personal style or fine writing style. It is not a quality that can be pinned down; no one style of dress or writing could suit every person or occasion. Finding one's own style or voice in writing can be incredibly difficult within the confines of academic writing (as we've seen in the last chapter) and certainly the classical rhetoricians did not seek to prescribe one. They did categorise three levels of style, however – low or plain, middle or forcible and high or florid – and devoted much attention to the pleasing effects of certain combinations of words. It was this consideration of the patterning of language for stylistic effect that resulted in a significant, enormous and still-growing classification system known as tropes and schemes (or figures). In short, tropes are instances when an individual word's use deviates from normal, while schemes refer to the artful deviation from the normal arrangement of groups of words. We will consider style in your own writing in chapter 5: Sentences, and the ways that a change of style can inflect meaning. It is worth noting here that within this rhetorical formula is the implicit suggestion that style is something distinct from the matter of an argument, like an ornamentation. We have already seen that this view was later challenged by Bakhtin, and by modernist writers and critics who proposed that form and matter are fused: they cannot be separated without causing alteration to one or the other.

Memoria and **Pronuntiatio** are both concerned with the delivery of the speech. Apart from stressing its importance, classical rhetoricians did not have a great deal to say about memoria since it means memorising the speech. As this book is concerned with writing, I don't have much to say about it either. When you are preparing a presentation for a seminar, learning it word for word, off by heart, may not be necessary, but it is of course desirable to be practised to a level where you can rely on a series of notes and prompts rather than reading from a full script. Pronuntiatio, delivery, can be improved by practice alone, and is one area in which the training of orators to vary volume and tone, to employ gestures and make eye contact, has remained consistent since classical times.

3.6.2 Tropes and schemes

The classification of artful manipulations of words is manifold; there are over forty types of schemes and more than fifty tropes (their definitions not necessarily uniform in the rhetoric textbooks throughout history). Some of the names will be extremely familiar to you, for instance, the tropes of metaphor and simile, the schemes of alliteration and antithesis, while others, for example, the words anacoenosis and meiosis, both tropes, are not used in everyday speech. However, while the Greek words themselves may only be found in textbooks, the practices to which they refer are more common. The rhetoricians were not designing methods of speaking but were classifying and giving names to the acts of transference (of meaning or arrangement) that they had found in existing speeches. Traditional students of literature, like the original students of rhetoric, were expected to identify tropes and schemes and consider their effects in poems and dramatic speeches, but, unlike rhetoric students, would not have then practised them in their own communications. This may still be the case for some students employing techniques of practical criticism; indeed, the study of certain schemes and tropes is particularly associated with poetic language, but it is a mistake to connect them more generally with rarefied literary forms since they structure so much of our daily communication: where would newspaper headlines be without puns (a generic trope for figures making a play on words) and alliteration (a scheme: the repetition of initial consonants in a sequence of words)?

Using tropes and schemes to read a literary passage

Here is the opening paragraph of the fourth chapter of Malcolm Bradbury's satirical novel *The History Man*. It describes the beginning of term on a university campus designed by a fictional Finnish architect, Jop Kaakinen.

> But now here it is, the day of beginning again, the day that is written down in so many diaries, and it is raining, and dreary, and bleak. It rains on the shopping precinct, as the Kirks do their early-morning shopping; it rains on the terrace, as they unload the wine and the glasses, the bread, the cheese, the sausages; it rains even on the University of Watermouth, that bright place of glinting glass and high towers, the Kaakinen wonderland, as Howard drives up the long carriage drive that leads to the centre of the site, and parks in the car park. In the rain, busloads of students arrive from the station, descending and running for convenient shelter. In the rain, they unload their trunks and cases into the vestibules of the residence buildings, into the halls of Hobbes and Kant, Marx and Hegel, Toynbee and Spengler. In the rain, the faculty, scattered over the summer, park their cars in rows in the car park and rush, with their briefcases, towards the shapely buildings, ready, in the rain, to renew the onward march of intellect. In the rain, academic Howard, smart in his leather coat and denim cap, humping his briefcase, gets out of the van, and locks it; in the rain he walks, with his briefcase, through the permanent building site that is the university, past shuttered concrete, steel frame, glass wall; through underpasses, down random slopes, along walkways, beneath roofed arcades. He crosses the main concourse of the university, called for some reason the Piazza, where paths cross, crowds gather, mobs surge; he reaches the high glass tower of the Social Science Building. He goes up the shallow steps, and pushes open the glass doors. In the dry, he stops, shakes his hair, looks around. The building has a spacious foyer; its outer walls and doors are all of brown glass; beneath the glass, in one corner, trickles a small water feature, a pool that passes under the wall and out into the world beyond – for Kaakinen, that visionary man, is a metaphysician, and for those with eyes to see, emblems of yin and yang, spirit and flesh, inner and outer, abound in his

futurist city. The foyer contains much bustle; there are many tables here;
at the tables sit students, representing various societies that contend, in
considerable noise, for the attention of the arriving freshmen. Just inside
the foyer Howard stands still, looking around; it is as if he is looking for
someone, seeking something; there is a task to fulfil.   (Bradbury 61–2)

This is a useful passage through which to see the way that rhetoric can be used
for comic and satirical purposes. The patterns of repetition here, the phrase,
clause and sentence structure schemes, known as *parison*, are pronounced. The
first sentence introduces a contrast which is then reinforced throughout the
passage, between high hopes and grim realities. The 'day of beginning again', a
phrase that we might associate with hope, is followed by the rather brutal *triad*
(or group of three) of 'raining, and dreary, and bleak' and in this contrast we
find the passage's governing technique. The effect is created by both schemes
and tropes. The phrase 'the day of beginning again' effectively substitutes for
more banal, less notable possibilities (the first day back, the first day of term)
and in doing so draws on a well-known convention in literary openings that
evokes imagery of new beginnings, of rebirth, spring, reproduction and
renewal. (An example is the opening of Chaucer's Prelude to *The Canterbury
Tales*, which describes the spring conditions that awake in pilgrims the desire
to go on pilgrimages.) This can be thought of as a trope, or a choice of phrase
that derives from a certain field of convention and meaning, but it is quickly
subverted by the gloomy triad that follows, which consists of the repetition of
three words with similar meanings. The effect is heightened by another repetition, of the phrase 'the day', which marks the items in a list of properties, and
even by the repetition of the word 'it', which refers to something hopeful in the
first half of the sentence and something grim in the second half. The repetition
of words and phrases becomes the most obvious technique through which the
passage goes on to develop its satirical atmosphere. In the first place, there is
the repetition of 'it rains on' that occurs three times, at the beginning of the
second sentence's three major sections. There is more to this scheme than just
this repetition. The *parallelism* extends to the next clause, in a structure which
repeats 'it rains on . . . as . . .' in all three sections. And there is more to the
pattern than that. The repetition of 'it rains on' is not perfect in all three cases,
since on the third occurrence there is a variation to 'it rains even on'. This is a
familiar rhetorical trick, which uses the triad to establish a pattern only to
break it on the third occurrence. (See, for example, Brutus's speech to the
angry mob in Rome after the murder of Julius Caesar in Act 3, Scene 2 of
Shakespeare's *Julius Caesar*, which makes use of the triad in this way throughout.) And we might ask why the scheme is varied in this way. The usual answer
will be that the element which deviates from the pattern is in some way

marked or foregrounded, and in this case it is apparent why that should be so. Why, we might ask, if it is raining on the shopping precinct and the terrace, should it not also be raining on the University of Watermouth? The implication of 'even', the word which does not belong in the pattern, is that the university might be exempt from the rain, with its glinting glass and high towers, as if its exotic pretensions might save it from the British weather.

The scheme then shifts from a repetition of 'it rains on' to a repetition of 'in the rain', the phrase that recurs six times in the next four sentences, not only at the start of each sentence but also within sentences, before transforming into 'In the dry' as Howard enters the Social Science Building. Taken together, the words 'raining', 'rains' and 'rain' are different versions of the same word, known in rhetoric as *polyptoton*. The scheme is doing more complex work than simply establishing the contrast between inside and outside in the passage. The rain continues to subvert the university's sense of itself, with its glass structures, its piazza, the intellectual ambitions of its halls of residence, and its aspirational architecture. The rainy bit of the passage also moves, in terms of its point of view, from a distant and general focus, to a more concentrated focus on Howard himself, so that the repetition of rain shifts also from a subversion of the university to a subversion of Howard himself. It is worth noting, too, the preponderance of triads throughout this description, but also the reliance that it continues to have on tropes for the construction of the contrast. There is, for example, the irony of the university's name, literalised comically by the rain, and then, when inside in the dry, the presence of a water feature, whose water passes under the wall and out into the pouring rain. The satirical purpose of the water feature must lie in the suggestion that this is a university designed for better weather. The contrast of the inside and outside, which the water feature also undermines, therefore functions in the structure of a contrast that is developed by the schematic structure of the passage's sentences.

Further reading

If you want to learn more about the history of rhetoric, schemes and tropes and their application to historical and contemporary texts from a variety of genres, Corbett and Connors's *Classical Rhetoric for the Modern Student* provides an exhaustive account; a briefer survey which introduces rhetoric as a means of structuring oral presentations is available in *Speaking Your Mind: Oral Presentation and Seminar Skills* by Stott, Young and Bryan; Bennett and Royle include a chapter on 'Figures and tropes' in *Literature, Criticism and Theory* which also analyses some literary texts and provides a guide to further reading on philosophical and theoretical approaches to metaphorical language.

3.6.3 From the Sophists to the present

Described in this way, the five canons of rhetoric appear as an extremely useful and practical guide to preparing a case and public speaking. Their democratic origins also cast them in a favourable light. Why then has the term rhetoric come to be associated with dishonesty? Part of the answer concerns a group of rhetoricians whose name has also become synonymous with fallacious reasoning designed to guile: the Sophists. The *OED* defines sophistry as the 'employment of arguments which are intentionally deceptive' but the men to whom the term Sophist originally was applied were a group of professors who taught rhetoric (Gorgias opened the School of Sophists in 431 BC). They did not teach sophistry (the intention to deceive) but the art of oratory as outlined above. The Sophists' schools, which charged fees, 'proved to be so lucrative that they attracted a number of charlatans into the teaching profession, and it was men like these who eventually gave Sophists an unsavoury reputation' (Corbett and Connors 491). However, the association of rhetoric with deceit is more deep rooted than this circumstantial explanation suggests. Implicit in the original Sophists' belief in the power of an eloquent speech to persuade, to make you believe, is a relativist world view, in which the notion of an absolute truth is surely undermined. It implies that instead of there being one absolute truth of a situation, existing independently of any account, if we hear another person's perspective we will understand that there are at least two sides to every story; for example, we have already thought about the way that Mrs Sellars's account of events in *The Children* might vary from Boyne's. It is this notion, that truth and morality are dependent upon circumstances and experience, that has contributed to the term's disrepute. It is an understanding of language, furthermore, that seems to have come full circle, as we have seen.

There is a distinction between the current practice of critics who seek to examine the rhetorical appeal of texts and the purpose of original rhetoricians that needs to be reiterated. The Athenians studied oratory forms in order to emulate their successful techniques. For them it was a given that all speeches, whether extracted from *poesis* (which we can loosely translate as poetry) or from, for example, a defendant's legal case, sought to persuade an audience of a particular point of view. They were not trying to uncover the point of view but to analyse the formula and the linguistic techniques employed to persuade so that they could use them in the future. Conversely, it was the aim of critics like Bakhtin and more recent exponents of cultural studies to discover the point of view, the ideology, that a text encourages its audiences to share, through a study of the language and style. In summary, the Athenians and twentieth-century critics both recognise that texts have audiences and that they seek to persuade their audiences of a viewpoint through particular constructions of language, but the object of the first group's study was the formula and methodology of persuasion, while the latter group are primarily concerned to discover what the audience is being persuaded. Both kinds of study have contributed to what we understand as the discipline of Literature. At a time when literary studies did not exist independently, the Sophists did not draw a distinction between the different genres; *poesis* and oratory were studied alike, neither was regarded more highly than the other. Similarly, contemporary theorists examine every form of discourse for persuasive techniques; this democratic interest in all utterances, from the elegy to the advert, has aroused suspicion and attracted condemnation from those who believe that the object of literary study is to create a hierarchy of texts (the canon), in which some are more valued than others.

Plato inflicted notable and lasting damage on the reputation of the Sophists. Belonging to a school of philosophy rather than rhetoric, his investigations into *poesis* sought a different outcome. He was not examining rhetorical or dramatic speeches as models from which to learn the skills of oratory but for what he perceived to be their relationship to reality. Plato thought of reality not as the concrete, visible world but as an abstract, underlying, general principle of truth. He thought that the concrete, visible world was already an imitation of this abstract reality, and so, when a poet or dramatist depicted something of the world in his speech, he was reproducing something that was already at one remove from reality. He thought of *poesis* as mimesis (imitation), famously excluding poets from his ideal society because of their practices of deception. He considered rhetoricians as similarly engaged with appearances rather than truth. His disdain for imitation was so strong that he even considered the written word to be a travesty; it was a copy of speech (the first employment of language) and it could be separated from its author. For Plato, the true was always the original. Although a high regard for the authentic may still have currency, you might find the idea that *poesis* (poetry) cannot access underlying truths surprising.

Response

Throughout literary history the distance that poetry stands from 'truth' has fluctuated. At times it has been held that poets have a more direct access to divine or spiritual knowledge and this view is still held by some. What is your view? Can you give examples? Does poetry differ from other literary genres in this respect? If so, how and why?

We can see that the contemporary contempt for rhetoric has its origins in Plato's thought but it was the intention of his pupil, Aristotle, to redress this. In *Rhetoric* (350 BC) he asserted the necessity of orators basing their arguments on what they believed to be true rather than an abstract notion of a universal truth. In *Poetics* (c. 330 BC) he suggested that poetry had special access to universal truths while other disciplines, namely history, dealt in specifics and were thus at further distance from universal truths than *poesis*. Unlike Plato, who disapproved of the influence of drama upon actors and audiences (another concern with a contemporary resonance, for he feared that they would be led into wrongdoing), Aristotle regarded dramatic characters more favourably precisely because they were not real but idealised people. He conceived that the ideal lay not in abstraction but in the potential that each living thing should aim for. It could be argued that Aristotle was an early exponent of a very early kind of genre theory because he identified that each species and genre of writing had its own rules and aims; everyone and everything was not to be judged against universal values.

Following Aristotle, there was another turn to the notion of an abstract and absolute truth in the writings of rhetoricians Cicero and Quintilian. Their work was to have a lasting influence precisely because its emphasis on the morality of the orator appealed to the clergymen who were largely responsible for education in the West from the seventeenth through to the nineteenth centuries. While Aristotle had stressed the significance of the audience in the triangular relationship of the orator, his speech and his audience, Cicero and then Quintilian, whose work has been irrevocably paired, foregrounded the necessity of the orator's moral discipline and education. The onus on the orator and the breadth of his education contrasted with Aristotle's belief in the necessary reliance upon available evidence in preparing a case. The lasting impact of the rhetorical theory of Cicero and Quintilian was not only its inflection upon the integrity of the speaker (where Aristotle rated the virtue of the effort), but in the furnishing of a full and diverse curriculum as the necessary training for such a speaker. The subjects that they recommended for study were the templates for the humanities subjects that undergraduates have read in the subsequent centuries.

Even a brief look at the history of rhetoric shows it to be an enduring and adaptable discipline. It initiated the formation of literary criticism and from the very start raised concerns about the possible moral effects of literature that are still hotly debated today. It has been crucial to the development of English Literature as an academic subject. It has, at different times, formed both the method and the object of literary study.

3.7 Wayne Booth (1921–2005) and *The Rhetoric of Fiction*

Wayne Booth's *The Rhetoric of Fiction* is a landmark in the critical understanding of narrative. First published in 1961, and selling well ever since, it is perhaps best thought of as a kind of summary of critical thought on fiction in the phase of American New Criticism. While the New Criticism is commonly associated with the close reading of poetry, as we have seen in the last chapter, it was in fact an era in which many of the major advances in the understanding of narrative and fiction were developed, and particularly through the analysis of fictional point of view. Booth's book is a brilliant demonstration of the analytical purchase of 'point of view' analysis, as well as a fascinating typology of narrative voices. For Booth, novels are very subtle in the way that they allow authors to control readers, offering to authors an enormous range of devices and voices through which the responses of readers to characters and events can be managed and manipulated. If anything, Booth seems to imply too much (perhaps too much for modern tastes) that narrative devices are all part of some brilliant calculation or intentional plan on the part of authors to produce particular responses in a reader, and, correspondingly, he tends to speak of 'the reader' as if these plans have the same effect on every reader regardless of who they are. This model of the novel as the successful control by an all-intending author of an undifferentiated readership is one that has been consistently challenged in narrative criticism since 1961, but the analytical resources that Booth develops in its service are among the highest achievements of narrative criticism and narratology.

Booth's analytical framework is based on the idea of a rhetorical choice made by an author of the voice in which a story is told. One such choice is that between the reliable and the unreliable narrator. This is a choice that normally defines the methods of control, or the rhetoric, of a particular novel. The reliable narrator, for example, is often an undramatised voice, whereas an unreliable narrator is typically a dramatised participant in the fiction. The reliable narrator, for example, might be the kind that knows everything about the story, and whose commentary we are to take as absolutely dependable. Such a narrator might also have the power to offer the reader an inside view of a character's thoughts and motivations, and this sort of access is for Booth a major rhetorical resource for the author. An inside view, Booth claims, reduces the distance between the reader and a character, creating an intimacy and proximity to one character that we may not have for others. In an analysis of Jane Austen's *Emma*, Booth shows the ways in which this proximity generates sympathy for Emma despite her faults, or to be more precise, the way that a narrator's movement in and out of the inside view can produce the careful combination of sympathy and distance which is required for the moral lesson of the novel to have its effect on readers. Booth shows that the moral judgement we make of Emma is determined by the degree of access and proximity we have to her thoughts, and that our judgement of her also depends on our being withheld from the minds of other characters, such as Jane Fairfax, from whose point of view Emma might look intolerable.

This example is just one of many forms of distance that operate in the rhetoric of fiction. Booth identifies various forms of distance that authors establish and abolish at their whim, as well as forms of distance that are adopted by readers of fiction: distance between the narrator and the implied author, between narrator and characters, between the narrator and the reader, between the implied author and the reader, the implied author and characters, and the aesthetic distance, as opposed to the uncritical proximity, that a reader may adopt from a work of fiction. The nature of the distance involved in these relations also varies: it may be physical, in the sense that the narrator may describe from a spatially distant point of view; it may be temporal, in the sense of distant retrospect; or it may be moral in the sense that the narrator may judge the moral character of the characters he narrates. It is in these relations that an author controls the distribution of information in a novel, as well as the reliability of that information, and the reader's access to it. Seen in this way, *The Rhetoric of Fiction* offers a model for the analysis of persuasion in general based on the disguise of authorial control and the principles of access to information and secret knowledge. Fictional narrative can be seen as a form of argument, as it has always been acknowledged to be in the structure of a sermon, which often presents a story before revealing the explicit argumentative purpose of that story, but it can also be viewed as a mode of discourse much more subtle, and less explicit, than argument, which controls our responses to topics and situations without our realising that it is doing so. In its ability to analyse these forms of control, *The Rhetoric of Fiction* establishes a basis of a view of literature as ideology, and of literary criticism as ideological critique.

Response

Can you think of examples of texts that have persuaded you to share a moral outlook that you don't in life? Perhaps through persuading you to identify with one protagonist above the others? Is this a feature of novels more than other texts?

3.8 More ways of discovering arguments

We saw above that a nineteenth-century teacher of rhetoric, George Quackenbos, identified inventio as the most difficult stage of preparing a case. I have suggested the folded-paper technique as one way of generating some ideas that can then be structured more formally into an essay or argument. Here are some more methods of questioning texts to discover their arguments.

3.8.1 The rhetoric of fiction: point of view

I suggested earlier in this chapter that the most important step you can take as a beginning literature student is one away from the text. Instead of allowing yourself to become immersed (at least on the second reading), you need to step back and consider how the text is beguiling you in this way. Here are some basic questions to ask a text in order to discover whose point of view you are being asked to share or identify with as you read, which can form the start of a deeper investigation into the text and ideology:

- Is there a story? What is it? If not, can you summarise the narration?
- Who is the narrator? Who is telling the story? Whose story or point of view is being conveyed? Where are they? Why are they telling the tale?
- Is there an audience within the text? Who do you think is the intended audience outside it (of the text as a whole)?
- Is there more than one narrator? What kind of a narrator is she or he? Are other voices heard?
- How might the events of the text be described differently by another person within it, or reader outside it?

Further reading

If you are interested in this approach to reading, you should explore stylistics and narratology. See, for example, Bradford's *Stylistics*, Weber's *Stylistics Reader* and *Feminist Stylistics* by Mills. Further reading on narratology can be found in the first chapter and you should also read Booth, of course.

3.8.2 The rhetoric of fiction: genre

Genres can be regarded as forms of persuasion. If this sounds a rather baffling proposition, consider a traditional romance, a Mills and Boon novel perhaps. The conventions of the romance genre lead us to expect the story to be told from the heroine's perspective. In general, and in the Mills and Boon romance in particular, we anticipate that we will identify with her quest for heterosexual love and that this search will be satisfied at the close of the narrative. (Interestingly, the format of the Mills and Boon novel is so prescribed that every one must have exactly 96 pages, enabling the knowing reader to calculate with accuracy their proximity to the agreeable resolution. If you scan the inside back cover of a Mills and Boon novel in a public library, you are likely to see a series of ballpoint hieroglyphics. Each individual symbol is the mark of a reader; the inscription enabling the voracious fan (or the person who visits the library on her behalf) to quickly identify novels that she's already read.) It is obvious that a genre sets up certain expectations; here I want you to recognise that these include point of view. You might like to consider the focalisation that you anticipate from different genres – and what happens when your expectations are confounded.

- Can you identify the genre of the text? Does the text belong to a recognisable genre?
- What implications does this genre carry about its story or purpose?
- Which protagonist/group perspective does the genre normally ask you to share? Which world view is embodied in this perspective?

Further reading

Frow provides an intelligent introduction to genre in his book of that title, while Duff's *Modern Genre Theory* is an anthology of recent theoretical writings on the subject.

3.8.3 Common themes

This activity is useful for grouping together texts that you have been studying. It asks you to list some themes and then to find references to these themes in the texts. It is a way of finding similarities and differences between them that may help you draw conclusions about the literature of, for example, a particular genre, movement or course that you are studying. The information that the completed grid reveals is dependent upon whether you read the rows or the columns: if you read the rows you'll find a range of comments upon a particular theme, whereas if you read the columns you'll gain a sense of what a particular text focuses upon or contains. You may also find that the grid helps you to choose essay questions and revision topics if you complete it week by week as you progress through a module.

	Source 1	Source 2	Source 3	Source 4
Common theme				
Common theme				
Common theme				

3.8.4 Questioning from a critical perspective

This section offers suggestions for the kind of questions that might be asked of literary texts by different critical schools or approaches. For further reading suggestions for each approach, please refer back to the outlines in the last chapter.

Feminism and Gender studies

- How does the text represent gender difference?
- Through point of view, or other means, does this text systematically exclude certain perspectives on gendered lines?
- Does the text call you into certain positions or identifications with characters on gendered lines?

Gay, Lesbian and Queer theory

- How is homosexuality represented in the text?
- Do existing critical readings of the text subdue its possible homosexual meanings and aspects?
- Has the text been neglected because of the sexualities depicted within it, or because of the sexuality of its author?

Marxism and materialism

- What material conditions (represented or unrepresented) underlie the social relations presented in this text?
- Does this text perform any kind of hidden ideological function, which is perhaps at odds with its manifest or explicit functions?
- What are the historical factors that determine the apparent individuality of characters?
- What industry does this text participate in?

New Historicism

- What are this text's contexts of production?
- What history does this text exclude?
- How can this text be read alongside non-literary texts of its period?

- What details does this text contain which signify an unrepresented social totality?

Psychoanalysis

- What does this text repress?
- What known psychoanalytical structures shape this text?
- How does this text represent neurotic disorders?
- In what way is the formation of identity or selfhood at stake in the text?
- Are there inaccessible or unconscious mental states that can be brought to the interpretation of the text?

Race, Ethnic and Postcolonial theories

- How is racial difference represented in this text?
- What is the relationship between aesthetic form and colonial history in this text?
- What history does this text leave out?

Reader-response theory

- In what ways is this text actualised by the reader?
- What are the factors that determine the reception of this text by an individual reader?
- What aspects of the meaning of this text are supplied by the reader?

Structuralism, Deconstruction and Poststructuralism

- How is this text structured?
- What are the hidden linguistic codes and conventions on which the meaning of this text depends?
- How does opposition function in this text? Are there hierarchical relations in these oppositions?
- What are the basic meaning-generating units of this discourse?
- In what ways can this text seem to be about itself?
- In what way does this text seem to resist or exceed efforts to impose single or coherent meaning on it?
- How does this text contradict itself?

Further reading

For more activities on how to generate ideas about texts that can form the basis of essays and arguments see Rob Pope's *The English Studies Book* and *Ways of Reading* by Martin Montgomery *et al*. For help with the direct application of critical theory to literature see Steve Lynn's *Texts and Contexts*.

Works cited

Andrews, Richard and Sally Mitchell. *Essays in Argument*. London: Middlesex University Press, 2001.

Bakhtin, Mikhail. *The Dialogic Imagination*. Ed. Michael Holquist. Trans. and ed. Caryl Emerson and Michael Holquist. Austin: University of Texas Press, 1981.

Bakhtin, Mikhail. *The Problems of Dostoevsky's Poetics*. Ed. and trans. by Caryl Emerson. Intro. Wayne C. Booth Theory and History of Literature, vol. 8. Minneapolis: University of Minnesota Press, 1984.

Bennett, Andrew and Nicholas Royle. 'Figures and tropes'. *Introduction to Literature, Criticism and Theory*. 3rd ed. Harlow: Longman, Pearson Education, 2004. 77–84.

Booth, Wayne C. *The Rhetoric of Fiction*. Chicago and London: University of Chicago Press, 1961.

Bradbury, Malcolm. *The History Man*. London: Secker and Warburg, 1975. London: Picador, 2000.

Bradford, Richard. *Stylistics*. London: Routledge, 1997.

Corbett, Edward P. J. and Robert J. Connors. *Classical Rhetoric for the Modern Student*. 4th ed. New York and Oxford: Oxford University Press.

Dentith, Simon. *Bakhtinian Thought: An Introductory Reader*. London: Routledge, 1995.

Duff, David, ed. and intro. *Modern Genre Theory*. Harlow: Longman, 2000.

Frow, John. *Genre*. London and New York: Routledge, 2006.

Lodge, David. *After Bakhtin: Essays on Fiction and Criticism*. London: Routledge, 1990.

Lynn, Steve. *Texts and Contexts: Writing about Literature with Critical Theory*. 3rd ed. New York: Longman, 2000.

Mills, Sara. *Feminist Stylistics*. London: Routledge, 1995.

Montaigne, Michel de. *The Essays: A Selection*. Trans. and ed. by M. A. Screech. London: Penguin, 2004.

Montgomery, Martin, Alan Durant, Nigel Fabb, Tom Furniss and Sara Mills. *Ways of Reading: Advanced Reading Skills for Students of English Literature*. 2nd ed. London and New York: Routledge, 2000.

Morris, Pam, ed. *The Bakhtin Reader: Selected Writings of Bakhtin, Medvedev, Voloshinov*. London: Edward Arnold, 1994.

Pope, Rob. *The English Studies Book*. 2nd ed. London and New York: Routledge, 2002.

Plato. *The Collected Dialogues of Plato, Including the Letters*. Ed. Edith Hamilton and Huntingdon Cairns. Princeton, NJ: Princeton University Press, 1961.

Stott, Rebecca, Tory Young and Cordelia Bryan, ed. *Speaking Your Mind: Oral Presentation and Seminar Skills*. Speak–Write Series. Harlow: Pearson Education, 2001.

Todorov, Tzvetan. *The Poetics of Prose*. Trans. Richard Howard. Oxford: Blackwell, 1977.

Todorov, Tzvetan. *Mikhael Bakhtin: The Dialogical Principle*. Trans. Wlad Godzich. Theory and History of Literature, vol. 13. Minneapolis: University of Minnesota Press, 1984.

Vice, Sue. *Introducing Bakhtin.* Manchester: Manchester University Press, 1997.
Weber, Jean Jacques. *Stylistics Reader: From Roman Jakobson to the Present.* London: Edward Arnold, 1996.
Wharton, Edith. *The Children.* New York: D. Appleton and Company, 1928. London: Virago Press, 1985.
Williams, Raymond. *The Country and the City.* London: Chatto and Windus, 1973. London: The Hogarth Press, 1993.

Chapter 4

Essays

4.1 What are essays for?

So far in this book I have emphasised that a key to becoming a successful English student is the ability to question things, or to no longer take norms for granted. This applies to the processes of studying as well as the texts and issues. In 1993, for example, Peter Womack, a lecturer at the University of East Anglia, decided to no longer take the essay for granted. He wrote a polemic in which he attempted to 'denaturalize the essay' for his peers, asking them to think about the reasons for its primacy in higher education.

> When we devise and teach English courses, we may have all sorts of educational outcomes in view – increased knowledge of a cultural heritage, enhanced sensitivity in reading, greater self-confidence in the presentation and discussion of ideas, social and cultural empowerment, personal maturity. But on the whole the only outcome we actually insist upon and evaluate is writing. Writing well – however this is defined – is the one thing needful for getting certificated in the subject; it's both the necessary and the sufficient condition.   (Womack 42)

Response

What are essays for? Consider Womack's assertion in the light of what you have read in this book so far, and your own experiences of being assessed in compulsory and higher education. Do you think that the focus on essays and writing detracts from the achievement of the other aims that Womack outlines? Should they be given more attention? Or have you found that in the period since 1993 teaching and examination at university has changed and Womack's emphasis doesn't match your own experience?

Womack is concerned that the use of the essay as a tool of examination establishes all other forms of writing and research at university as preparatory, that is, part of the build-up to essay writing rather than valid activities in their own right. Ultimately he is arguing for radical changes in the composition of essays and their use and purpose in academia – chiefly campaigning for collective production and against 'current administrative functions' that insist 'on individual authorship' (Womack 48) – but he also celebrates the essay as the best means of expressing a polemic, including his own, to a wide audience. In fact, having something to say, an argument, a polemic is crucial; no essay will succeed if it does not make a case. I have tried to suggest that through your reading practices and writing your log, for example, you should devote much of your writing time as a student to activities other than the essay but I have also insisted that you shouldn't start writing an essay until you have undertaken these many other activities of reading, research and composition of arguments. Like Womack, I would encourage academics and students to undertake different forms of writing and research activity and to work more collaboratively but I also agree that the essay can have positive functions of expression; in this chapter we will consider exactly what an essay is and how to write one.

4.2 What is an essay?

Response

Make notes on exactly what you think an essay is. What does it look like? How long is it? What kinds of material does it contain? Can an essay be written on any subject? Where are they written? By whom? What kinds of language and tone are used?

You probably agree that an essay is a coherent piece of prose writing of between 1,000 and 5,000 words. (The length probably depends upon which stage of your degree you are at, with shorter essays at Level 1 and longer ones in the final year.) They are written on many topics but predominantly found in schools and universities. They usually answer a question and are composed of sentences and paragraphs – you'd be surprised to find an essay that was written in verse or as a series of fragments, and, in fact, tutors are often alerted to problems that the student has had with structure and coherence of argument – or absence of an argument entirely – from the layout of an essay that is written in one huge chunk, or conversely, countless isolated sentences. We've already stated that an undergraduate essay should have an argument and, as you may have mentioned, that this argument should be supported with evidence from texts and experts. It is generally perceived that to give the argument credence it should be logical and written in a formal register; it should be specific and not over-generalised. You might reasonably expect an introduction to the essay's subject and to the way the essay will approach it at the start, and a conclusion (to the same) at the end. Last but not least, you would expect an essay to be free from typographical, spelling and punctuation errors.

4.2.1 The five-paragraph essay

In high schools in the US, it is still customary to find that the recommended essay structure has five parts (similar to those outlined by Corax that we discussed in the last chapter). Known as the 'five-paragraph essay', this document has only five paragraphs, unsurprisingly: an introduction that sets out the topic, three paragraphs each with a subtopic that supports the main one, followed by a summary that powerfully restates the argument and concludes the essay. If you search the web for 'five-paragraph essay' you will find many pages that use hypertext to state the designated purpose not just of each paragraph but of every sentence in examples of the five-paragraph essay.

Response

Look at a website that presents the structure of the five-paragraph essay such as www.geocities.com/soho/Atrium/1437 or www.gc.maricopa.edu/English/essay/.
Copy or make a plan of the five-paragraph essay. What are the strengths of this formula? What are its weaknesses? How does it build an argument? What is missing from the content of this type of essay? Have you ever written an essay to such a tightly structured plan?

Although school students in the US are examined on their ability to write a five-paragraph essay, its *raison d'être* is purportedly to give practice in basic writing skills that will lead to future success in more varied forms. Detractors feel, however, that writing to rule in this way is more likely to discourage imaginative writing and thinking than enable it. The five-paragraph essay is especially suited to what are known as expository and narrative rather than argument essays, that is, essays that simply describe something rather than make a case. You may have noticed in your analysis that, unlike Corax's tabulation, the five-paragraph essay utilises only *supporting* evidence. It does not include the material or argument that develop a critique of the main premise and that are demanded in the five canons of rhetoric or perhaps in a more sophisticated essay. By including and analysing perceived oppositions within your essay, you show awareness of your reader and strengthen your case by anticipating and refuting, or at least discussing, their objections. The five-paragraph essay is less aware of its audience and sets out only to present information, an account or a kind of story rather than explicitly to persuade the reader.

Response

What are the intellectual consequences of only providing supporting evidence for your argument?

4.2.2 The features of an undergraduate essay

No one at university is going to recommend that you adhere to a scheme as rigid as the five-paragraph essay (I hope) but there are certainly features common to all successful undergraduate essays that we can identify as the first step to practising them in our own work.

Response

Read the essay in the Appendix. It was written by Alex, a student in her first year of study for a degree in English and American Literature at the Open University. Make notes, using specific examples from her prose, against this broad checklist of the desirable features of an essay:

Does it

- contain an argument?
- answer a question?
- contain evidence from texts? If so, what kind of texts are they? Literary, historical, critical or theoretical?

Is it

- logical?
- formal?
- specific rather than generalised?

Does it have

- an introduction?
- a conclusion?
- paragraphs?

Is it free from

- factual errors?
- typographical and spelling errors?
- errors of punctuation?
- errors of presentation? (For example, failing to give references for quotations, failing to double-space or leave a margin, etc.)

The tutor who marked Alex's essay did not give it a specific grade but indicated that it was of borderline Upper Second / First Class standard. For this high mark we would expect it to contain a strong argument, with a good understanding of the texts, well supported by evidence and all communicated in clear and correct English, but perhaps not to demonstrate the original thinking or highly developed command of relevant theory or context that would be expected for the highest marks.

4.2.3 The marking criteria for an undergraduate essay

In their student handbooks, module guides or on websites, most English departments provide their students with the marking criteria for essays. These are checklists of features that tutors use to analyse and grade essays and are more detailed than the broad list I gave above. They vary slightly in different establishments but the ones I have reproduced below from the English Department of Anglia Ruskin University will give you a fair impression of what your tutor will be looking for when she or he marks your work. (Note that the numerical mark does not make use of the full range – only exceptional students attain 80 per cent or above – but in some institutions and for certain assignments this is not the case and 100 per cent is an achievable grade.)

Numerical mark	Class of degree
70% +	First Class Honours
60–69%	Second Class Honours, First Division (a '2.1')
50–59%	Second Class Honours, Second Division (a '2.2')
40–49%	Third Class Honours
Less than 40%	Fail

First Class work

First Class work is intellectually excellent and demonstrates some, or all, of the following qualities:

80% +	• Exceptional and consistent deployment of all qualities defined in the 70–79 category, with an outstanding degree of originality.
70–79%	• Perceptive and sometimes original thought and a clearly structured argument, well directed to the question.
	• A penetrating level of analysis fluently at ease with the topic.

- A focus on the full implications of the question asked and a sophisticated awareness of associated problematic issues.
- Careful organisation and cogent, progressive argument.
- Clear and articulate expression.
- The work shows a breadth of reading, fully supported with relevant and detailed evidence properly documented and referenced.
- Command of relevant theory and contexts.

Upper-Second Class work

Work in this class demonstrates some of the qualities listed above under First Class work but not in as sustained a way. Upper-Second Class work is very good work, but it is not intellectually outstanding. In varying degrees of strength it demonstrates some, or all, of the following qualities:

60–69%
- Good powers of analysis systematically deployed.
- A thorough treatment of the topic.
- Clear, accurate and sustained address to the question.
- A developed argument.
- A good, literate use of English.
- Use of detailed supporting evidence.
- A good command of relevant theory and context.

Lower-Second Class work

Work in this class is of good, and not merely passing, Honours standard. Such work is characterised by some, or all, of the following qualities:

50–59%
- Reasonable powers of analysis, but of a less developed and enquiring level than work of Upper-Second Class standard.
- A sound treatment of the topic, but probably omitting some key points.
- Partial answer to the question.
- The argument is not fully developed. The work often depends rather heavily on secondary reading or lecture notes.
- A satisfactory, but sometimes imprecise, use of English.
- An inconsistent use of supporting evidence.
- A satisfactory command of relevant theory and context.
- Sporadic, over-generalising or unfocused analysis of specific texts.

Third Class work

Although weak, work in this class is of passing Honours standard and should not be confused with failed work. It demonstrates some, or all, of the following characteristics:

40–49%	• Limited power of intellectual analysis.
	• An inconsistent focus on the topic.
	• An evasive, or poorly directed, address to the question.
	• The argument is undeveloped and often shows heavy reliance on plot summary and/or paraphrase. Assertions are insufficiently substantiated with evidence.
	• A pedestrian, and frequently repetitious or inaccurate, use of English.
	• A limited knowledge of the text and little detailed reference to it.
	• A marginal command of relevant theory and context.

Failed work

There is a wide range of 39 marks for work that is not of passing Honours standard, from 0 per cent for failure to submit work to 39 per cent for a narrow fail. The full range is used as carefully as possible to indicate the extent of the failure and the work's closeness to being of passing quality. Failing work will show some, or all, of the following weaknesses:

0–39%	• Negligible or feeble power of critical analysis.
	• A lack of focus on the question asked.
	• A failure to answer the question.
	• No developed argument. The work contains logical errors or fallacies and bad or confused organisation.
	• An ineffective use of English. Failing work will probably demonstrate incoherent syntax, bad spelling and word choice, and wrong punctuation.
	• A poor knowledge, or extensive misunderstanding, of the text.
	• No awareness of relevant theory and context.

Reproduced by kind permission of Anglia Ruskin University

Response

What are the main differences between First Class and failing work?

You may find that you can broadly summarise these features under three headings: argument, knowledge of text and context, and use of English. Alex's essay clearly demonstrates ability in these areas. Her argument is supported by the detail given throughout the essay but is also articulated in the opening and closing paragraphs. She argues against the quotation in the title, claiming that even if social reform is not explicitly stated in the slave narratives, this is still both their intention and their result. Her familiarity with text and contexts is revealed in her confident tone as well as her examples and she has a good command of written English.

4.2.3 Spot the difference: a failing essay and a First Class essay

It is often easiest to perceive strengths and weaknesses through comparison. Here are two authentic extracts from first-year essays; the question asked for a consideration of gender in Robert Louis Stevenson's 1886 novella *The Strange Case of Dr Jekyll and Mr Hyde*. (They are reproduced verbatim; I have not made any corrections.)

Introduction from essay 1

Jekyll and Hyde was a book based on Robert Louis Stevenson's own experiences, especially with middle-age men in Edinburgh and London. What he knew best about that milieu becomes the driving force for of the novella. This world was where façade counted. The cut of one's suit, the social status of one's friends. Above all this was a world of appearance not substance.

The whole basis for this novella could be construed as strangeness in itself. There are few women characters.

In 'the story of the door' there is the character Mr Enfield. Instead of being an interesting story of a strange door, a mystery has evolved and both Mr Utterson and Mr Enfield have more questions, rather than less, about Jekyll, Hyde and their relationship.

Introduction from essay 2

Robert Louis Stevenson's *Dr Jekyll and Mr Hyde* is a text that shows little sign of the female emancipation that was occurring at the time in which it was written. Instead it maintains gothic misogynistic themes wherein women were either demonized or marginalized (in Stevenson's case, both), as a response to their increasing sociocultural threat to the male hegemony. In the first scene we are treated to a recollection by Mr Enfield of seeing a young girl 'of maybe eight or ten' (Stevenson 1987, 9) being trampled on the street by Hyde at three o'clock in the morning. Within moments Hyde is surrounded by women 'wild as harpies' with 'hateful faces' (Stevenson 1987, 10) trying to attack him, with only Enfield and a doctor preventing them from doing so. Next we are presented with the image of a maid fainting upon witnessing the murder of Danvers Carew. Later whilst searching for Hyde, Utterson and Inspector Newcomen come across his landlady in Soho who has 'an evil face, smoothed by hypocrisy' (Stevenson 1987, 27). Finally we are presented with the 'hysterical whimpering' (Stevenson 1987, 42) or Dr Jekyll's cook and housemaid who upon Utterson's arrival at the calamitous scene, cries 'Bless God!' (Stevenson 1987, 42), at this seemingly divine intervention. By sparsely populating the narrative landscape with these Victorian archetypes, Stevenson not only marginalizes women but compounds the culturally damaging gender identities that are propagated within them.

Doane and Hodges (1988, 70) re-enforce the subtext of threatening behaviour toward the male patriarchy from the 'new woman'. They note that when Utterson and Poole eventually break down the door to Jekyll / Hyde's library they find inside a conventional and cosy domestic scene. However the angelic and obedient housewife who, according to Victorian gender prescriptions, would traditionally exist within this setting, has been transposed by Stevenson with that of the monstrous Hyde and his 'contorted and twitching body' (Stevenson 1987, 49). Doane and Devon (1998, 70) see this as suggestive of the 'terror and division threatened from within the home – the angel was now the demon in the house'.

Response

Make notes on the differences between the essay extracts. You could use the classification guidelines above to award each essay a mark, if you like, and write a report for each student that kindly summarises their strengths and weaknesses.

I have recorded the actual marks awarded for these essays at the end of the chapter but I am sure you had no difficulty in identifying which failed and which was designated First Class. Firstly, the appearance of the work is quite different; essay 1 is composed of short disjointed sentences and paragraphs while essay 2 consists of two dense paragraphs visibly containing quotations and references, patterns that were repeated throughout the whole of the essays. On reading the first extract, I am not sure what the argument is or where the essay is going to take me. The student hints at quite a promising argument – that the key to *The Strange Case of Dr Jekyll and Mr Hyde* is indeed 'strangeness' – that in more confident hands could have been developed fruitfully, especially with reference to queerness and homosociality. And there are other promising features of essay 1; although it has not been proof-read – 'for of' – it does not contain spelling or punctuation errors. However, on the whole it is confusing and fails to introduce the reader to its argument, the novella and its contexts. (Note how it assumes knowledge of the text; there's no introduction to the characters or the fact that the chapters have different titles such as 'The Story of the Door'; we'll discuss appropriate levels of descriptive information later.) Essay 2, meanwhile, is highly confident, demonstrating awareness of the period in which the novella was written – 'female emancipation' – and of literary genres – 'gothic' – right from the start. Its argument is clear: *Jekyll and Hyde* seems to reveal the fear of the 'new woman' through its absence of female protagonists and depictions of female stereotypes at the margins of both the novella and society. This argument is demonstrated with close references to the text and with quotations from appropriate critics. The vocabulary of this extract is broader and more interesting than that of the first; the writer also employs more sophisticated sentence structures.

4.3 How do you think you write an essay?

We have looked at some essays now, thought about what a good essay should look like and what it should (and shouldn't) contain. Now we are going to turn to the processes of preparing for and actually writing an essay.

Response

In as much detail as you possibly can, make notes on how you write an essay.

- When does this process start for you? When you are given a deadline or essay questions or at some moment before this?
- When you have completed this plan, describe how you think an essay *should* be written.
- Which aspects are missing from your own previous practice? Which parts of the process are you confident about and which areas do you feel require development? Now would be a good time to gather some of your own essays and analyse their strengths and weaknesses. Which areas have your tutors praised? And where have they suggested areas for improvement? Make a list of aspects that you would like to develop.

4.4 The stages of writing an essay

The structure of this book roughly follows the first broad stages of rhetoric that we saw in the last chapter: inventio, dispositio and elocutio. We have considered reading, research and the structure of argument before we turned to arrangement, the writing of the essay. It's clear that this procedure also makes sense when thinking about the final processes of writing an essay: you think about the question, research it, then arrange and write it. But this structure is still too vague and commonplace to be very helpful – and, in fact, I have gone some way to suggesting that you should consider yourself researching at all times and not only after being presented with an assessment question – so when you turn to the many essay-writing guides available, you'll find that they break down the process into anywhere between around three and ten stages. Often these stages relate to the actual writing of the essay itself, rather than the whole experience of studying for a module, selecting a question and researching it, etc. However, I have identified seven crucial steps which most experts would agree on, which incorporate the whole process: (1) thinking of or about the question, (2) research, (3) making a plan, (4) the thesis statement, (5) writing the main body of the essay, (6) beginnings and endings and (7) editing. You may be surprised at the order of this sequence and you are free to experiment with it. I am not proposing a drill like the five-paragraph essay: indeed, the process of writing an essay may follow a circular rather than linear movement with the repetition of some of these steps. Now we are going to look at each one in more detail.

4.5 Thinking of or about the question

In some universities, as I outlined in the first chapter, you'll be examined on a topic at the end of a module by answering one essay question from a list that your lecturer has determined. In others you may write more frequently and/or to questions that you have composed yourself. Whether selecting or writing an essay question, you should proceed with care; a significant number of essays are unsuccessful because they don't answer the question, are unrelated to the question, misunderstand the question or, even, are bored by the question. There are as many pitfalls in choosing a 'safe' question as in choosing a 'difficult' one. If you feel extremely comfortable with a topic, it can be easy to give a rather stale and predictable answer that perhaps won't fail but may not inspire your reader; it's also possible that in perceiving a question as simple or straightforward you may be missing something.

Choosing a question Here's a simple question to ask yourself before you think about your assignment: which of the texts that you have read on your course stands out? This is not a question about which texts you like, or which you have enjoyed; it could be the reverse, the answer may be a text that you've found difficult in some way. (Examining why you or other readers and critics have found a text's structure or morals incomprehensible, for example, can be extremely productive.) If you have an answer to this question, then you should rule out any assignment that will not enable you to explore it.

A common formula of essay questions is a quotation – sometimes from an identified source, sometimes not – with a question, 'Do you agree?', or injunction to 'Discuss' at the end. As with provocative texts, if there is a quotation that you feel strongly about, then you have made your choice. You should always try and write about a topic that will sustain your interest through the long process of researching and writing about it. This is important to remember when you are faced with a range of questions that cover topics you are uncertain about. Again, I'd advise you not to shy away from difficulty automatically; often an attempt at a less 'mainstream' question may be rewarded for its originality and the novelty of researching something new can be inspiring. It is probably more productive than offering a formulaic answer to a question that most of your peers have answered. (Now may be the time to put yourself in your tutor's shoes: imagine she or he has to read forty or more scripts; thirty people have answered the same question but ten have volunteered essays on other topics. Would you rather yours was the twenty-ninth script on the same topic or the thirty-fifth essay your tutor reads that happens to be on something new?)

Understanding what a question wants As I have said, and you may have noted, questions tend to follow a common formula. They usually contain two kinds of key words that we can call key *topic* words and key *request* words. Your first step to knowing what a question wants is identifying the key topic words or phrases. What do you think they are in the following question? **'The sight of women dressing as men on the Elizabethan stage was unsettling to audiences because it denoted the attempt of women to claim patriarchal power through the donning of male clothing. It is thus a different issue from that of male transvestism on stage.' Discuss.** If you failed to consider 'women dressing as men', 'the Elizabethan stage', 'patriarchal power' and 'male transvestism', it is hard to see how your essay could answer this question. The key topic words clearly relate to the subject of your module (here Elizabethan drama) but there are a limited number of key request words – *discuss, compare, in what ways does . . .?, give examples, explore, analyse* – that appear on every assignment sheet. But despite this variety of terms, very few literature assignments will demand only *illustrations* of a particular feature: however the question is phrased your tutors are looking for 'knowledge transformation' rather than 'knowledge telling'. This means that they do not want you to simply *list* all the examples of cross-dressing on the Elizabethan stage, for example; rather, they want you to transform this data into a case about power, gender roles, sexuality and representation in the seventeenth century.

One method of finding an argument in every essay question is to look for what, for the sake of shorthand, we will call the *opposition* that is either explicit or implicitly contained within it. Here are some examples of essay questions and the oppositions contained within them:

'Modern Britain, like the ancient civilisations, seems to view the opposition of city and country in moral terms with the city as the site of corruption, sexual transgression and godlessness, and the country as a harmonious pastoral ideal.' Discuss with relation to at least two texts from the module. This essay question, taken from a first-year course on contemporary British fiction, is explicit in its binaries. The quotation sets up a clear distinction between the city (immoral) and the country (moral) while proposing continuity between the opposites of past (ancient civilisations) and present (modern Britain). There are several ways in which it invites you to use the course texts to demonstrate or to refute the oppositions. One way of exploring this would be to draw two columns, one headed 'City' and one headed 'Country'. You could then list the associated terms under each heading along with notes you've made during your own reading on the course texts. Having examined critical and literary texts you might find that, for example, (1) the opposition between urban and rural life is and always has been false, but representations of the city and country continue to perpetuate the dichotomy; or (2) the opposition between urban and rural life may have had validity in the past but in an era of globalisation and mass communications, people's lives share a high degree of commonality and so this distinction can no longer be drawn. Of course, there are many other arguments you could make and this is hinted in the question's key term 'discuss'; being asked simply to 'agree' or 'disagree' with the proposition could lead you to the false assumption that this is a closed debate with a clear yes or no answer. The arguments will depend upon your chosen texts and your interpretation of them. It's also worth noting that a binary is a scheme of classification in which one side of the duality is often perceived as positive and the other as negative and this value system may be something that you'd like to challenge in your essay (for example, the idea that morality and immorality can be so starkly defined and mapped onto geographical locations).

Here is an example of a question, from a third-year course on seventeenth-century writing, which contains its opposition more implicitly:

Write an analysis of one of the texts we have studied this term situating it in its historical context, and showing both how history illuminates the

formal properties of the text, and how the text illuminates its historical context. If you were to underline the key topic words of this question, it's likely that you'd highlight 'text', 'historical context', 'history' and 'formal properties'. You could begin your analysis of the question, and therefore construction of your argument, by collating notes in two columns headed '[name of chosen] text' and 'historical context', perhaps considering that the text's 'formal properties' and 'history' could be included respectively underneath them. But the question suggests not a straightforward opposition but a reciprocity between text and context, or even a triangular relationship between three things that have been or are considered to be distinct: the text, its context and history. Exploring the possibilities of this question would definitely be assisted by drawing freeform diagrams. The difficulty of assigning your notes under two headings could be the activity that leads you to produce your argument.

Response

Take an assignment sheet from a course you are currently studying and see if you can find oppositions in its essay questions. What are the possible arguments that you could make from them?

Writing your own question Even if you can or must compose your own question, much of the advice above still applies. It's vital to choose an area that will interest you during all the processes of completing the task. If you are bored when writing it will show, and no tutor wants to read an essay that is stale and uninterested. You should write a question that won't encourage a simplified answer to a complex issue (try writing a question that you don't know the answer to), that won't request only illustration rather than an argument, and preferably one that takes an unusual approach rather than adopts a very familiar or tired stance. You can employ the 'quotation plus question' formula; this may help you to keep focused and is easiest if you have been making notes when undertaking the initial stages of research, or keeping a reading log; you can refer back to the words of a writer that were especially apt, succinct or intriguing.

If you are devising the title for a longer project, such as a dissertation that could be between 8,000 and 10,000 words, don't immediately assume that the larger word count necessitates a much larger topic. It is a common mistake for students to imagine that a dissertation requires a heading as broad as: 'Discuss the representation of women in nineteenth-century fiction'; they fear running out of things to say. But it is far better, when faced with a longer project, to consider a topic in more *depth* than in more *breadth*; you will only make generalisations if you try to give blanket coverage to a substantial subject. Here is an example of a dissertation title that also considers gender in nineteenth-century writing: **'View my wasting skin'** – **consumption, irregular eating and the cult of the thin woman in mid-Victorian literature**. Not only is it more focused but it is also much livelier and enticing to the reader; its concentration upon the key terms relating to weight, illness and a narrower period of fiction gives the impression that the author is confident and knowledgeable. Once again, the importance of being specific cannot be overemphasised. Limit your topic to a very precise era, movement, author, genre, narrative or poetic structure. One way to help you to do this is to consult the MLA bibliography in order to see the approaches critics have recently taken to the subject that you have broadly decided to write about. This is an index that lists all the articles, books and chapters in books that have been published year by year on literatures and linguistics. You search for a key term and it lists all the citations for that term, title or author. You can see http://www.mla.org/bibliography for more information but you should also be able to access it through your library's web-pages. Alternatively you can look at *The Year's Work in English Studies* for a paper version of work published on language and literatures in English (or search it online at http://ywes.oxfordjournals.org/). (MLA stands for the Modern Languages Association and is an American organisation, while the YWES is published on behalf of the English Association which is British, but both indexes are international in scope.) Awareness of the latest research will give your own writing a freshness and relevance that will impress your tutors and make your work stand out.

4.6 Research

As I have argued above, much of the work that falls under this heading should have been completed before the last activity. Throughout this guide, I have urged you to make notes and structure arguments around literary and critical texts as you read. It is far better to approach essay questions with some arguments and ideas about the texts than wait to respond to a question and to take your lead from it. Your response is more likely to be genuine, interesting, individual and unformulaic. However, you will need to gather the material and notes you do have and to supplement them with further reading that is geared towards the assignment you've chosen. And even then you may find that the process of essay writing does not continue in a linear sequence but causes you to write a paragraph or even a draft and then return to research to advance or refute a point you had not anticipated making. First, we'll consider the notes that you already have.

4.6.1 Taking notes from lectures

Attending lectures is one of the features of university that is different from school. We saw in the last chapter that a lecture is the occasion when a lecturer presents information and a point of view about a specific topic relating to the module. In most institutions, going to lectures is not compulsory, but to miss them is to miss out on hearing about not just your subject but the particular focus of the subject as it is being taught on your course (for example, a lecture on the fiction of Katherine Mansfield could focus on the modernist style of her writing, her situation as a colonial writer in London, or a feminist reading of her stories). The ability to present a good lecture is a skill and so, perhaps surprisingly, is the ability to listen well. It's all too easy to drift off into a daydream, or even sleep, and then to discover that the hour is over and you've barely heard a word. This is why lecture theatres have uncomfortable seats. No, this is why lecturers are recommended to use audio/visual aids and to provide a clear structure and 'signposts' to stimulate their audiences and it is the most important reason why you are encouraged to take notes. If a lecture lasts an hour, it's obvious that you won't remember every detail without a record but the other reason for note-taking is, chiefly, to enhance your own listening skills. We saw in chapter 2 that reading is not a passive activity and here we must also learn that successful listening is similarly active.

How to take notes at a lecture

Find out what the lecture is about You should be given a programme at the beginning of the course that lists all the titles of the lectures and what you'll be studying in the seminars. If a lecture is going to be on a particular text, then make sure you read the text *before* rather than *after* the lecture. This way you will already have some idea of what the lecturer is talking about when she or he mentions particular characters, themes, motifs, etc. If a lecture is more generally on a period, movement or theory, for example, then ask the lecturer if there is a critical text you could read in order to familiarise yourself with the topic beforehand. Without familiarity with the points of reference, the lecture could just sound like baffling gobbledegook, and you cannot always rely on the lecturer to define her or his terms (particularly after the introduction to the course); this is your responsibility.

Make sure you have a pen and paper, or laptop It's an obvious point, but your ability to concentrate on the lecture will be impeded if you fear your ink is going to run dry or you run out of paper. (Some people record lectures, particularly if they have problems such as dyslexia that make it difficult to write notes at speed; it's customary to ask permission before using audio equipment to record someone else's words.) Here's another obvious point: if you arrive late or in the wrong room, you'll have missed the all-important introduction and will be so hassled that you may find it impossible to catch up. If you have followed the first step above of familiarising yourself with the lecture's topic, then at least if you arrive in the wrong room you'll soon know about it, unlike the two engineering students at my university who sat through twenty-five minutes of a lecture on 'Reading Poetry' before apparently realising their mistake.

Listen for signposts and use any handouts that you've received The main problem with a lecture is that you can't control the speed or volume of the lecturer's delivery and so you are never going to be able to record her or him word for word. Even if you had this capacity, it might not be the best way to make notes since you would still then have to sift through them for the salient points. Instead, you want to begin the process of analysing the lecture as you write it down – another reason why listening to a lecture is an active rather than passive skill. It is to be hoped that your lecturer has provided the bones, the structure of the lecture on a handout or displayed on a screen for you to see. You should write your notes around these headings. But even if she or he hasn't provided a visual plan, the lecturer will use verbal 'signposts' to structure the lecture and indicate when an important point is to be made. These 'signposts' should act as little jolts to your concentration, alerting you that something significant is about to be said. They include phrases such as: 'I'm going to discuss three main points',' the second point is. . .', 'in other words', and 'to conclude'; if you have the same lecturer repeatedly you'll begin to recognise his or her favoured phrases for indicating the lecture's key points.

Develop a system of abbreviations As I have indicated, even if it were possible it would not be profitable to record the lecture word for word. Don't even consider attempting to record whole sentences. You are aiming to make as many notes as you need to be able to reconstruct the lecturer's argument and evidence at a later date. So you need to group your notes under headings (that will probably have been provided by the lecturer) and to develop your own shorthand and abbreviations for writing at speed. There are many ways of doing this. It's worth bearing in mind that rsrchrs hv dscvrd tht ppl cn stll mk sns f wrds whn thy'v hd thr vwls rmvd. (And you may already know this from the process of text (SMS) messaging.) You should use symbols wherever possible, developing your own for words that come up frequently in the study of English (for example, I have my own quick symbol for the word 'character' and use the conventional ones for 'men' and 'women'). Remember that lecture notes will never be assessed; you can experiment with your methods of taking them and feel free to record them as spider charts, diagrams and not necessarily linear sequences. But do make sure that you have a heading on each page of notes with the title of the course, the lecture, the date, the lecturer's name and your own name for your own filing system (and so your notes can be returned to you, should you lose them).

What to do with your notes You've left the lecture hall and moved on to the next class or out for a coffee with your friends. It's all too easy to imagine that your work on the lecture is complete. In fact, if you've gone for that coffee, now would be a good time to go through your notes to see if your fellow students have recorded things that you missed and vice versa, and to discuss if there are issues that you didn't understand that you'd like to raise collectively with your tutor. Whether you undertake this as a group or on your own, you must spend time going through your notes as soon as possible after the lecture. There are things that make sense as you jot them down that in one day's time will be incomprehensible. Now is the time to flesh them out while the lecture is fresh in your mind and you still have a chance to check out things you didn't understand with your lecturer. This is also the time to decide on the questions raised in the lecture that you'd like to pursue. The lecturer will have referred to ideas, texts and critics that you can read about now in preparation for seminar discussion and, later, essay writing. Finally, make sure you have a sensible filing system; a folder for each course, perhaps. Don't just abandon your notes in a scruffy pile that will be difficult to sift through.

4.6.2 Making notes in a seminar

This is a bit more problematic than making notes in a lecture because the primary purpose of a seminar is to have a group discussion. If you focus on taking notes, you'll find it hard to join in the conversation and to raise the issues you think are important or require clarification. Conversely, if you are fully engaged in the debate then it will be impossible to record what is being said simultaneously. You may have experience of seminars in which people frantically jot down every statement that is uttered as a way of avoiding participation; if you keep your head down in the process of note-taking the tutor will also be unable to make eye contact with you and you won't feel compelled to contribute. But this is an unproductive situation; it can leave a few individuals feeling resentful about being lone spokespersons but, more importantly, will mean that the full range of interests in the seminar room will remain unexplored. It's entirely understandable that you may feel afraid of speaking out because you're worried about saying something stupid but, as I have stressed above, the seminar works best when it is an open forum where people feel able to ask questions and not just deliver wisdoms. The chances are that if you are uncertain about an issue, you won't be alone and your peers will be extremely grateful to you for broaching it. I explained above that one way to conquer potential embarrassment is to work with a group of peers, ideally after a lecture, to decide on points you'd like to share and debate. There is another reason why individuals don't speak out in seminars and this is the feeling that an idea is so good they don't want others to 'steal' it. This is a perhaps understandable but flawed way of thinking. Firstly, if you proffer your idea it is likely to be developed or critiqued by your peers in ways that you have not considered and you can feel pleased about directing the debate. Secondly, even if everyone recorded 'your' idea in his or her essay it would not mean that your grade would be any lower (and in any case this is not likely to happen). Thirdly, we've seen in chapter 2 that ownership of ideas can often be contested; how will you know how original your idea is until you share it? Given that you are likely to have only about ten hours' contact time each week (at most) with your tutors and fellow students, it is vital that these hours are not spent in silence as you closely guard your inspirations or fear making a fool of yourself.

Response

What is your experience of seminars so far? What do you expect from your tutor in a seminar? What kind of participant are you? Do you find it easy to contribute? Or do you have a tendency to dominate? One way to avoid both extremes might be to set yourself the resolution of asking three questions in every seminar.

It's true that some tutors make it easier to speak than others. To return to the issue of note-taking, the most helpful lecturers will be the note-takers themselves in the seminar room. If they record key words on a whiteboard, perhaps as a kind of spider-diagram, as the group speaks, this will form a record that you can quickly copy during or at the close of the session. Alternatively, or in addition, your tutor might spend the last ten minutes summing up what has been said. If this is not the case in your current experience, ask your tutor if it might be a possibility. Both the end-summary and the ongoing spider-diagram are simple ways of enabling a record to be made without conversation being stilted. Again, it would be highly productive to share notes after a seminar with your peers or to go through them afterwards to fill in the gaps. This would be a good time to go to the library to find texts that will enable you to pursue the ideas that have inspired you during the seminar, while they are still fresh in your mind (and before others get to the library first and borrow the relevant books).

Response

If you have ever had to summarise a seminar discussion or a lecture to a friend who was absent you'll know that this quickly reveals how much you've understood and recalled, how much you've missed and forgotten. After your next lecture and seminar, try to explain the key points to someone from your course who wasn't there. What kind of questions did they ask you? What have you learnt about your own note-taking from this activity? How will it affect the way you take notes in the future?

How to use your lecture and seminar notes when preparing your essay

We are now returning (or moving forward?) to the stage when you have your neatly filed folders of notes from lectures and seminars. (These may have been supplemented by your further reading as a consequence of the seminar and by the notes you made when undertaking primary reading beforehand.) You have scrutinised the assignment questions for their key topic words and perhaps identified one or two that you intend to write about. Before you systematically go through your files to find how and where these key terms are replicated, it's worth at least mentally listing their synonyms; it won't always be the case that the exact phrases come up in your observations and you need to be aware of the bigger issues that are being hinted at. It probably goes without saying that if you are considering a question like the one on seventeenth-century writing above, it is unlikely that simply looking through your notes for the name of the text you're going to analyse and the words 'history' or 'historical context' will be at all productive. Instead, you are looking for occasions where you've considered the form of the text itself and jotted down historical events and the names of historians that relate to the period of its production. However, if you've been looking at more theoretical texts, it is likely that the words 'history' and 'form' may themselves come up. I would recommend highlighting the different topics in different colours, so that when you return to your annotations you can quickly pinpoint relevant areas. At the very least, undertaking this exercise will tell you how prepared you are already, or, if you come up with a blank, that you should either start researching or turn to an alternative question or text. Inevitably there will be large swathes of your notes that now go unhighlighted, for no essay question will ask you to analyse every component of every text on the course and no answer should seek to do so. Some people find that this is their particular essay-writing difficulty: working out what to exclude. At this stage, it is not too great a problem to have too much to say, but if you have highlighted all of your files, it's likely that you are not focusing specifically upon the key topic terms, or perhaps that the key topic terms are too broad. If everything you and critics have observed about a text seems to relate to gender or its form, say, then it is up to you to try and limit the terms. But this will happen either as you undertake new research specifically for the essay or at the next stage when you construct your argument and thesis statement.

4.6.3 How to undertake new research specifically for your essay

We've thought a lot about reading in this book already, as you might or might not expect in a guide to studying literature. You might not expect it, because it might be a skill that you take for granted, as we've seen, but I have stressed that reading at university is quite different from reading for leisure: for a start, you must read with a pen in your hand. But there are still several different purposes for reading when you're studying English. We are now at the stage where you have already read the key texts on your course once and are beginning to consider what kinds of extra reading and material you'll need to write your essay about them.

Close reading the key texts You should always reread the primary texts that you have chosen to write about, to stand back and consider how their effects are achieved. If, for example, you are reading a novel, then, on this second reading, you are not looking to see what happens or allowing yourself to become immersed in the story, but thinking about the text's meanings and attempting to discover how they are created. You may wish to annotate the original texts and should certainly highlight quotations, patterns and features either on the book itself (assuming you haven't borrowed it from the library), perhaps on a photocopy if it is a shortish text, or with the use of post-it notes. (For questions to ask to analyse a work in this way see the end of the last chapter.) You might wish to use a system of colour-coding for this activity, too, highlighting each theme in a particular colour and formal features in another. Remember, using different colours for verbatim quotes and for your own ideas makes inadvertent plagiarism much less likely to occur. And again, the one thing that you don't want to end up with is a block of text that is completely highlighted in a monolithic fashion, suggesting that you have not been able to distinguish its noteworthy aspects. (Incidentally, if you do find that using colour is helpful to you, develop your own system that you use consistently, always using red for issues of form, purple for issues of gender, etc.)

Starting to make some connections Now you might want to start linking the texts as one precursor to identifying an argument (this is following a strategy of inductive logic). A Venn diagram can be very helpful. Each circle that you draw represents one of your key texts. In the central shared area, you note the features that they have in common, while in their independent segments you record their unique features. This will prompt you to consider probable and possible explanations for the shared features and for the differences, be they to do with form, genre or theme. You have now generated some claims and could indeed write an essay based on these ideas alone (although you will not have demonstrated 'awareness of the relevant theory and context' demanded by the criteria above). Your answer is likely to be fuller and free from inaccuracies if you take steps to interrogate your suppositions. So now is the time to begin secondary research. You may be looking for methods of analysing genres, narratives and aspects of form, historical or contextual information, critical theories to evaluate texts from the perspective of feminism, Postcolonialism or Poststructuralism, for example.

Reading for facts or ideas Research has shown that there are two types of reading: for surface or for depth. Reading for surface is like reading for facts that will remain unquestioned by the reader. It's likely that this type of reading does take place more often in other subjects but it certainly has a place in literary studies. For example, in a course on suffragette writing, you may be interested in discovering the timeline of female emancipation around the globe but once you've discovered that women in New Zealand first gained the right to vote in 1893 you are unlikely to spend further time musing on whether this date is accurate or not. Reading for depth, meanwhile, refers to this questioning attitude of mind; 'deep' readers are not simply seeking bald facts but are looking beyond them to analyse their meanings, and the ideas and frameworks that lie behind them. The deep reader would not devote time to verifying the accuracy of the dates but might question why all adult women in the UK did not gain the right to vote until thirty-five years later than those in New Zealand, for example. The deep reader will constantly attempt to place *all* the material and knowledge she or he finds in relation to the rest. This is the kind of active reading and thinking that will lead to a more accomplished essay. In the essay extracts that we looked at above on *The Strange Case of Dr Jekyll and Mr Hyde*, we can now see that essay 2 was written by a deep reader. That author had identified the types of female character in the novella and related them to patriarchal fears of emancipated women at the time it was written. The author of essay 1 was more of a surface reader; she or he had recognised that the novella was about strangeness but had not placed this into a wider context. So, although you may have recourse to some surface reading you should ensure that you train yourself to undertake deep reading predominantly.

Books, articles or the Internet? Currently, many lecturers devote a lot of time to moaning that students don't read books any more but only surf the Internet for the first relevant page they can find. We've already discussed that, yes, there is a lot of unedited rubbish on the web that you'd be a fool to rely on, but also noted that there are some very worthwhile sites that will give you access to scholarly articles, archives and texts that you would not otherwise be able to get hold of (and I indicated some of these above and in chapter 2). Sometimes, using electronic resources can be the only way to access up-to-date material; your library may have more journal subscriptions online than in paper copy. And the advantage of this is that journals may be easier to search using key terms than if you had to wade through the indexes of paper versions.

Old or new? Here is one way of broadly categorising the types of critical material that are available to you: classic volumes that may have been composed at any moment in history but that all contemporary critics still respond to; and recent articles or books that contemplate a topic from a viewpoint or critical stance that could not have been imagined at an earlier time (like eco-criticism, for example). Between these two poles are texts that may have become outmoded but without gaining the classic status of the first group; you should try and avoid relying upon these as your primary critical resources. It's likely that 'old' texts on your reading lists are there for a reason; if you are unsure about whether other 'old' books that you come across are worth reading or have been made redundant by subsequent criticism, then check with your tutor.

To read or not to read? Whether you are browsing an abstract (a short synopsis of a book or article) on an online index, or picking up books from a library shelf, you still need to employ good judgement in deciding whether or not, or how far, to read on. You can waste a lot of time reading too far around a subject, perhaps because of a lack of confidence in putting pen to paper or perhaps because it feels like a valid diversionary activity to prevent you from putting pen to paper. But it is rarely the case that you will need to read a whole book for an assignment, although you'd be unlikely to read less than the whole of an article for it to make sense. So how do you decide what to read?

First, consult your reading list, the library catalogue and the MLA bibliography Again, I am assuming that you are at the stage of having already undertaken the preliminary generalised reading for your course. You have now started to focus on a more specific question or two, and have identified the key topic words from these questions. If you are scanning an online search engine then insert these key terms and hit 'enter' to see what you come up with. This is likely to be productive since, hopefully, your tutors are aware of the main debates around an author, movement, era or group of texts etc. If nothing – or too much – appears, then attempt some lateral thinking and try again with related terms. Your librarian will help you individually, or run workshops, on making the most of online searches and this is a skill worth practising. If you were working on the question above about representations of rural and urban life in contemporary Britain, typing in 'godlessness' or 'ancient civilisations' would result in far too many hits that are irrelevant to the precise context in which you are considering them. It would be far better to type in the titles of the contemporary texts, their authors or film directors, and then once within a relevant document to insert words related to the city, sexuality and religion, etc. There will always be a certain amount of trial and error in this process and you should be prepared to spend some time investigating all possibilities. (This can be an enjoyable and enlightening experience in itself; certainly the more you do it, the more likely you are to search with accuracy.) The same process applies to searching the library catalogue, or the contents page or index of a book you've picked up. Of course, the more well-known the author the more selective you will have to be. If you are researching a topic for a module on Shakespeare the resources will be endless, so you'll need to ascertain your key topic words with greater precision, while looking for articles on the forgotten modernist Hope Mirrlees will only result in one or two results and thus you'd expect to read them all.

Skim read Browsing in the library in this way is one occasion when the ability to skim read is an advantage. Skim reading your key texts is not advised, as you will miss the nuances that precisely enable you to understand how it makes its points, but glancing superficially over pages of a secondary text to pick out relevant information, and, indeed, discover whether the text is useful at all, will save you a lot of time. There is no need to feel obliged to stick with a book, even if you found some of it to be relevant. Be ruthless and stop reading once its discourse strays from your topic.

> **Note** When you have found a relevant article, passage or chapter from a book, it is still a good idea to make notes from it rather than just photocopy or download it. Owning a copy of the complete text is like owning the transcript of a lecture; it is still a dense mass of information that requires careful sifting for gems. The danger of possessing the whole text is that you feel that your work is done, rather than still waiting to be done.

4.7 Making a plan

Now you have lots of notes from your lectures, your close rereadings, and your secondary research. (It might be an advantage at this stage to have made them on loose leaves of paper rather than in a bound notebook, so you can shuffle them around and place them all in front of you on the table, or even the floor.)

You should arm yourself with blank sheets of paper and coloured pens in order to visualise the points of similarity and difference, support and opposition, for the case you hope to make. However wedded you may be to your computer, it really is a good idea to work with pen and paper at this stage because you are aiming to make all sorts of links and connections that can be indicated through arrows and bubbles that are free to loop around your page, in multiple directions if necessary. You want your ideas to flow rather than be constrained by the linear logic of the word-processor.

The first thing to do is to review the claims you made after constructing your Venn diagram. Have they gained credibility or been refuted by the reading you've completed subsequently? Don't worry if the answer to this question is not straightforward. When we considered argument in chapter 3 we favoured the kind of dialogic approach considered by Bakhtin, which means that regardless of the manner in which a question may be phrased (demanding a yes or no answer), for most questions around literature, any response may be more contingent (by which I mean it is dependent upon the critical perspectives you have taken and the texts you have read, etc.). Now you should attempt to visualise your findings through a diagram once more, this time one that will have a more complicated and unique structure.

grounds (the evidence from your Venn) → claim → support (from further reading)

↓

rebuttal (from further reading) → new claim

This is an imagined segment of what could be a huge chart. Remember, at the moment, you are only roughing out ideas, your final essay plan will emerge from these trains of thought but you do not need to record them in the sequence in which you hope to write your final essay. This is more of a brainstorming session, although one that is not entirely freeform but composed from your existing notes. We saw earlier that the five-paragraph essay had quite a simple structure. Here we are attempting a more advanced version, one that considers qualifications and rebuttals (opposing evidence or views), and not just supporting evidence for your claim. Structuring your notes in this way may lead you to refute your original claims, to provide new or additional ones. (Although your original claims may have become somewhat discredited during your extended research, it might still be fruitful to incorporate them in your essay as part of a final argument that challenges what is apparently obvious upon first reading.)

In this methodology that I have outlined so far, we have been following a kind of inductive reasoning that has generated claims out of particular features found when comparing your primary texts (as discovered through the Venn diagram). I have been emphasising this course of action, where you have already formulated strong ideas about the key texts before approaching the essay questions but, of course, you may prefer to follow a deductive practice: one that starts with the claim and then looks to key texts and secondary research to support or refute it, i.e. moving in the opposite direction from large claims and general principles to the smaller details. Whichever way you have conducted your enquiries, the plan of your essay will still look the same. Your introduction and conclusion are going to outline and propose the claims and the body of your essay is going to be composed of arguments and evidence that support and refute them.

I have suggested that the process of finding arguments can be a meandering one and even that an essay may be dialogic and open rather than come to an absolute and final answer on a subject. However, this does not mean that your essay should be composed of every single thought you've had on your texts, and without order. Your reader will need to be guided through your thoughts so that she or he can at least understand what the debates are. So now that you've made your diagrams of claims, evidence, questions and counterclaims, you must think about pruning. Look again at the question and now consider how relevant all the material that you've gathered is. Be bold and delete (at least for the purposes of this assignment) everything that is not absolutely germane. This can be hard. You may feel that you've made some really original and interesting connections but, if these don't relate to the question, they will not enhance your essay but divert your reader from the issues at stake. (If you really feel that your best ideas are not pertinent to the question, perhaps you should see if there's another question that will provide a natural home for them.)

So you need to transform the meandering structure of your diagram above into a schema that more approximately resembles this formula from classical rhetoric (see top of next page).

These sections do not straightforwardly correlate to paragraphs. The claim could be your single-thesis statement (see below); or a smaller component of your discussion relating to a specific text or author, for example, that will help build your overall argument and may be combined with the supporting evidence in one paragraph; or the supporting evidence may span several paragraphs. It is thus quite likely that you will repeat sections (2) to (6) or (3) to (6) and you will have to do so if you have split an essay into two halves, one on each key text or author, for example. These components may also be sandwiched between a separate introduction and a conclusion and we'll consider these below, although the information contained in the first box, the issue, could serve as an introduction. I hope you've noticed that throughout the

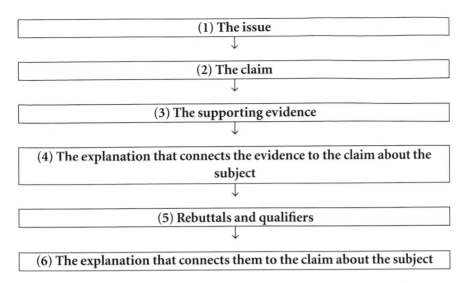

reading, planning and additional research stages of this essay-writing process, the ability to make connections and to make these explicit in your writing is crucial. They will be the links that hold the chains of your argument together, as well as the proof that you are a deep and not a surface reader.

Response

I have presented the essay above as a series of linked boxes. This is to help you realise that an essay is a sequence made from individual components not one long splurge of free writing. This realisation should remove some of the fear from writing; if you concentrate on the building blocks, you will find the construction of the whole edifice occurs without you even noticing.

Take an assignment that you are currently working on and write a plan based around these blocks. Don't worry if each block is not the same length and, remember, this is not a five-paragraph essay, so you may have to repeat some of the stages, particularly those that provide further examples of or rebuttals to your thesis statement. The idea of presenting these blocks from classical rhetoric is simply to encourage you to break down the stages of your argument, not to suggest that it must be rigidly adhered to in this order.

4.8 The thesis statement

The idea of the thesis statement may be new or something familiar to you depending upon whether your education so far has followed an American or

British system (remember seeing the thesis/thesis statement featured in the five-paragraph essay guides above?). A thesis statement is like the claims that we have discussed above but it is the claim that you have finally refined as being the guiding principle of your essay. It is important that you decide upon it before you start writing the main body of your essay; it should act like a magnet, attracting all information that is metal to your argument and repelling all that is not. By this I mean that you should write down your thesis statement on a small separate piece of paper, stick it to the top of your word-processor and check every paragraph you write against it for relevance. If your writing does not offer support or rebuttal to your thesis statement, then press delete.

How to write your thesis statement Remember, your thesis statement is a sentence-long summary of your argument. You are not aiming to describe phenomena but to account for them. Recall all the representations of nineteenth-century women that we have encountered in this chapter. If we were to guess the thesis statements of our sample-essay extracts, we'd find that the first one was a *description* – '*The Strange Case of Dr Jekyll and Mr Hyde* is about strangeness' – while the second gave an *argument* – 'That the women in Stevenson's novella are represented as stereotypical figures on the margins of society indicates the fear of female emancipation that was occurring in society at the time.' Your thesis statement is an argument that you are going to examine with recourse to evidence from primary and secondary research.

4.9 Writing the main body of the essay

By now you have a sequence of boxes loosely based around the diagram above. Each box will contain an idea and some page references to quotations from literary and critical texts that support or refute the idea. You are ready to write your first draft of the essay. At this stage your aim is to write out in full the contents of each box. This is a draft so you don't need to worry too much about introductions and conclusions, individual word choice, sentence structure and links between sentences and paragraphs; you will revise these later. So what kind of information do you need to include in these building blocks of your essay?

Summarising texts and arguments Most guidebooks to successful writing emphasise the importance of knowing your audience. In this you have an advantage supposedly (you know that the audience for your essay is your tutor); however, this knowledge can feel more like a problem, and not only because your tutor is probably reading your work to grade it. The problem can be working out how much to tell your tutor. On the one hand, you are being asked to explain or expound upon a topic but, on the other, you are being asked to do this to someone who probably, or inevitably, knows more about it than you do. This assumption causes difficulty when you consider how much background or summary information you need to present. We saw an example of this when we considered the two *Jekyll and Hyde* essay extracts. The one that failed provided no synopsis of the novella. Quite understandably its author assumed that the tutor would be highly familiar with the text and so omitted an account of it. However, you should always give at least a brief summary of a text to indicate your own knowledge of it, so how can you work out how much information is the right amount?

There are two things to bear in mind. Firstly, if the text you are discussing is not a set one and is perhaps something you have independently researched, it is worth giving more information, for your tutor may not be familiar with it. But whether or not the text is set or independently chosen, you should always use your introductory synopsis, be it a sentence or a paragraph long, as a way of underlining your thesis statement. In the terminology used above, your knowledge should not be *told* but *transformed*. In the First Class essay on *Jekyll and Hyde*, the description of the plot was an account of the stereotypical representations of women in the novella; in Alex's essay, Equiano's slave narrative is introduced in the fourth paragraph in terms of its structure, narratorial position and register underlining the paragraph's main idea that this text became a model for other slave narratives. If you inflect your account in this way, you will never be guilty of simply presenting information to your tutor that she or he already has. Instead you will inform her or him of your critical position – perhaps with the support of other critics – and provide evidence for the overall argument of your essay.

Using quotations and critical texts The correct way to present short and long quotations will be explained in chapter 6: References. Here I wish to point out that you should never include free-floating quotations. They must always be embedded in a sentence, if short, or indented in a paragraph, if long. Sadly, I cannot present a magic breakdown indicating the correct ratio of your words to literary quotations and the thoughts of critics, but I will say that the majority of words should be your own. If, when you look back at your first draft, you find it to be a collage of quotations that, if highlighted, would result in pages that are more colourful than white, then you need to cut and rephrase. On the other hand, if you were to find no colour were you to undertake this exercise, then you need to return to your notes to provide more evidence from sources outside your own head.

4.10 Beginnings and endings

The very definitions of these words imply a place in the sequence of essay writing that is contradictory to the one I am suggesting: surely the introduction should be written first and the conclusion last? In fact, it makes far more sense to write them both when the rest of your essay is completed. At this stage you know precisely what it is that you have said and thus what you want to introduce and conclude. When you first start writing, although you have your thesis statement, it's still likely that the weighting eventually given to particular issues and examples will be different from that which you planned. Introducing the essay once written will allow you to be precise and confident about what is to follow.

Introductions and conclusions perform an important function; their roles are always emphasised in guides on essay writing. But they are notoriously difficult to compose, leading students to resort to simply repeating the question in their introductions, for example, and at the end to try and condense a range of responses into one glib concluding sentence. Personally, and possibly controversially, I would rather read an essay without an introduction or conclusion than one that starts 'In this essay, I will consider [words from the question]' and finishes with the phrase 'In this essay, I have shown that [words from the question.]' These are boring statements of the obvious that just eat up precious words from your limit without telling me anything. Below I suggest some alternative ideas.

Response

Look at examples of your own essays. Have you provided introductions and conclusions to each one? Have these been genuine introductions and conclusions to the subject or simply words repeated from the question?

4.10.1 Beginnings

The start of an essay is the place where you must address but, as we have seen, not just repeat the question. It is the place where you provide an overview or some context of the issues that the question raises but, most importantly, it is where you introduce your argument. This might involve the verbatim inclusion of your thesis statement although you may wish to reserve this for your conclusion and simply outline the issues at stake here. It would certainly be helpful to introduce your critical approach and you can declare which texts you'll employ to discuss it. But this is *not* the place to provide a biography of the author or, despite what you might be told, the time to present dictionary definitions of the words in the question. Unless these terms have contentious or huge and vague meanings, such as 'ideology', for example, you do not need to provide an explanation. And, if they do require clarification in order to demonstrate your precise understanding and deployment of them, then use a literary dictionary or glossary of theoretical terms to indicate their use in a literary or critical context, or to explain whose account of 'ideology' you share; often, even the *OED* will not contain definitions of words as they have been used in the discipline. It is a good idea generally in this presentation of the scope of your essay to employ critical support; this will not only clearly indicate your own critical position but will give your reader confidence in the research that is to follow.

Just as your tutor provides signposts in a lecture, the introduction to your essay is a way of signposting what is to come. This can lead to some rather repetitious phrasing such as using 'In this essay I will show . . .' to begin a sequence of sentences. Although your reader, your tutor, is obliged to read your essay, it still helps to open in a style that is attention-grabbing. This means using varied sentence structures and phrases as well as presenting striking information and the argument of your essay. If this still sounds daunting then remember the advice that I started with; brevity is far better than a rambling account of a broad topic or regurgitation of the title.

Response

Look at the opening paragraph of Alex's essay. Of the features I have described above, which has she included? Has she omitted anything you'd expect to find in an introduction? Do you think it is successful? What is her argument? How does it relate to the question?

4.10.2 *Endings*

Here is a helpful statement about conclusions: you are only concluding your own essay, not the whole of the issue that it is concerned with. Remember the Bakhtinian notion of dialogic exchange? Think of it when you finish an essay, because any attempt on your behalf to provide a final concluding statement to a large topic will inevitably result in something reductive and oversimplifying. Instead, in your conclusion you are drawing your own thoughts to a close and possibly indicating the futher issues that your essay has raised. If your assignment question can be answered 'yes' or 'no' or has an 'either x or y' structure, you might expect that the sensible way to end your essay is with a clear statement agreeing with x or y and employing a sentence like, 'This essay has shown that on the Elizabethan stage female cross-dressing was nothing to do with male transvestism on stage.' But as with the introduction it is far better not to parrot the question's words; furthermore, you need to show that you have demonstrated the complexities of the topic and not just perceived a straightforward opposition. Now is not the time to include interesting new information that a reader will wish you had chosen to explore in the main body of your essay, but it is acceptable to suggest that there is an ongoing debate, or that your conclusion offers only one critical perspective, for example. The over-assertion of one point at the close of an essay can tarnish the reader's memory of what has been an otherwise intelligent and discursive piece; you want your reader to go away thoughtful, musing on the possibilities you've illuminated.

Conclusions: some tips

- You are only concluding your own essay, not the whole of the topic.
- Avoid reductive, oversimplified statements that attempt to conclude the whole of the topic.
- You are reminding the reader of what you have argued throughout the body of your essay and weighing up this, your own, argument.
- You can suggest alternative possibilities that you haven't had room to consider but make sure this is not a long list of interesting features that the reader will wish you had devoted your essay to instead of the things you actually wrote about.
- Your aim is to leave a good impression; don't ramble. If you read the introduction and conclusion of your essay do they strongly indicate what comes between? If not, then revise them until they do.

4.11 Editing

The temptation to hand in your essay the minute you've finished it can be compelling. You feel such relief at having completed the task and perhaps also a slight embarrassment at the thought of what you've written, that the desire to never look at it again can be overwhelming. It *is* a good idea to put your work to one side for a couple of days. (Have you noticed how much time you need to write the best essay you can? It is a process that, in its entirety, should take weeks.) Nevertheless, even if you don't have this much time, you should put your essay aside for at least a few hours, but then, I am afraid, you *must* return to it.

There are several reasons why you must put some distance between yourself and your essay and then review it as though you were a new reader and not the author. Things that were clear to you as you wrote them (because you've been privy to every step of the process) may appear confused or impossible to follow. When editing your essay you need to consider it in several different stages. Firstly, you must read at the macro level, that is, reading the whole essay to judge if it has an argument and makes the case clearly, then you can progress down to the level of paragraphs; does each one coherently support the essay's assertions? Next, check each sentence for clarity and grammatical accuracy (we'll be looking at some of the most common errors in the next chapter) and also for overly repetitive sentence structures. It can really help at this stage to read sentences aloud; even if no one is listening you'll be surprised at how muddled or meandering your phrases can seem when you enunciate them. The final step before proof-reading is to analyse word choice. Have you overused certain words? Are you sure that you understand the meaning of words in this particular context and that they are appropriate? It is a good idea to use a thesaurus, if you find you've overused certain terms, but you must ensure that, in the specifics of a literary essay that demands close attention to words above all else, you have not substituted an inaccurate or unsuitable word for a tired one. Don't use your thesaurus without simultaneously consulting a dictionary. As a tutor, I can often tell when a student has reached for the thesaurus without fully checking that the swapped words are appropriate; it can give a flavour of an essay written by someone whose first language is not English and leave me puzzling over individual words rather than the overall essay and argument.

At each of these stages, you may need to stop and undertake serious revisions. This is one reason why working on a computer rather than writing by hand has made life much easier; you can play around with drafts, deleting passages or switching the order of paragraphs. It's worth remembering that no professionally published text (I am discounting self-published work on the web) is a first draft. All texts are read and edited by peers or whole teams of editorial staff, each checking for different components. Why should your writing be any different? There are a number of things that might need revision. You might find that at a temporal distance certain links in your argument no longer make logical sense. This could be at the level of a sentence or the structure of the whole essay. It is a good idea to go though your essay and consider how well, or even if, the paragraphs and sentences connect as links in a chain. However, you might still feel too close to your own writing to detect lapses in logic and connection. Ideally, you should show your work to someone else whose fresh eyes will spot them. In some institutions, particularly in the US, it is the practice to submit a draft of an essay to your course tutor before the final one that will be graded. If this is not the case at your university, there might, in the US, still be a member of a Writing Center, Study Skills Center or, in the UK, a Royal Literary Fund fellow, who is authorised to undertake a reading of your drafted work and to offer assistance with revising it. You could work with a fellow student and organise an arrangement where you read each other's work before submission to look for 'problems'. I can see why you might feel wary or intimidated about doing this, especially if you haven't experienced any 'peer review' work during the course of your study, but one way to make this less daunting would be to do it with someone who is on a different course or in a different year; this may alleviate the element of competition. (I should note, I am not encouraging the crime of 'collusion' here, where you both jointly write and submit the same work. This practice carries similar penalties to plagiarism.)

> Finally, a word of caution: once you've redrafted your essay, you must go through the process of editing it once more. One strong reason for this is because in the cutting and pasting or rephrasing, argument can end up out of kilter. At sentence level, the subject that may have been denoted by a pronoun may have moved so the topic is no longer clear. (If you're unclear what a pronoun is, turn to the next chapter.)

Other things to look out for when editing

Tautology This word indicates repetition but can be identified as a fault in your writing for two reasons. Firstly, it can be the unnecessary repetition of meaning: some commonly used examples are the phrase 'this annual event held every year' and 'free gift'; since 'annual' means 'held every year' the remainder of this phrase, after 'event', is superfluous; in the second phrase, a gift is by definition something that you are not expected to pay for, so the word 'free' is tautological and unnecessary. Once you start to look for them, you can find many occurrences of tautology in everyday life – how often have you heard someone say 'at this moment in time' instead of simply 'at this moment' – and as we can see from these instances, tautology can indicate a lack of attention to individual word meanings; in an essay it would waste precious words from your overall limit. Sometimes tautology is used to good effect: the phrase 'boys will be boys' and the song lyric 'que sera sera, whatever will be will be' are successful in conveying a weary or satisfying inevitability. There is another kind of tautology that is more of a problem for essays, though; it is the presentation of the same information as both the cause and the effect of a point in your argument. For example, in an essay on the treatment of single women in women's writing between the wars, I found the following sentence: 'Single women were described as *surplus* women because there were so many spinsters after the death of men in the first world war.' This statement posits the same information (that there was a high number of single women) as both the claim and the supporting evidence (and certainly does not question or transform the notion of superfluity in anyway).

Logical fallacies and non-sequiturs Non-sequiturs are occasions where a statement or inference does not logically or thematically follow on from what has gone before (within a sentence, or in a sequence of sentences). They are quite a common mistake in student essays. If the non-sequitur relates only to theme, for example, in the puzzling sentence 'Charlotte Brontë fused gothic and realist styles in her novels and was the sister of Emily Brontë', where there is no apparent connection between her writing style and her sibling, then the damage to your essay overall might not be serious (although it does suggest a confusion about the aim of each sentence or paragraph and the sequence of ideas). But a non-sequitur relating to logic can create a fallacy that might derail your whole argument. This occurs when an observation is made and you read on thinking that a principle is going to be drawn from it, but in fact the rest of the sentence or paragraph is not a consequence or is even unrelated. There is a whole branch of logic devoted to the different categories of fallacy (with about two hundred different varieties). These are broken down under two headings, of formal and informal fallacies: a formal fallacy is one where the argument is flawed and the principle that has been deduced from the evidence is incorrect, while an informal fallacy is one where the flaw lies not in the reasoning but in the facts. Correcting such fallacies or non-sequiturs may therefore mean inserting some information that is currently missing, or removing information from the sequence, but it may also involve a more drastic rethink of the thought processes that led to your original deduction.

Links (or lack of them) In order to guide your reader smoothly through your essay, your argument and your mode of logic, you need to ensure that paragraphs link to each other and within them, so too the sentences. At the end of each paragraph you need to conclude it and also introduce what will follow. There are some very clumsy ways of linking paragraphs and these should be avoided. Phrases like 'in order to answer this point, it is first necessary to . . .' are overly wordy and are a heavy-handed way of attempting links.

Response

Reread Alex's essay in the Appendix and highlight every linking word with a coloured pen (things like 'however', 'moreover', 'on the other hand', 'because of this') and underline every sentence that forms the link between one paragraph and another. Are there occasions when you feel the link is not clearly made? If so, how would you have changed this?

Response

As you read the essays of your peers and critics, make a list of linking words and phrases. Collate these under two headings: one that suggests that additional information is to follow (for example, 'furthermore') and one that suggests that an alternative viewpoint or contradictory information is to follow (things like 'In contrast').

A checklist for editing your essay

- **Argument** Can you identify your thesis statement from the final essay? Does each paragraph provide further support, or clearly analyse opposing views to this argument? Would some of the evidence or information assist your argument if it was moved to a different place? (Remember to save each draft as a clearly marked file so that if you wish to revert to an earlier order or remind yourself what you have cut etc., you can easily do so.)
- **Evidence** Have you provided evidence in the form of quotations and your own paraphrases from both critical and literary sources? Remember that your essay should be more than just a mosaic of other people's thoughts, though, so the editing you need to do may be cutting this supporting evidence rather than adding to it.
- **Paragraphs** Does each one contribute to the essay's assertions? Do they follow on logically from one another?
- **Links** Have you linked your sentences and paragraphs? Have you done this using varied words and phrases?
- **Sentences** Read your sentences out loud to see if they are clear and make sense. Have you used a variety of sentence lengths and structures? We will look at varieties of sentence structures and their implications in the next chapter.
- **Word choice** Again, have you used a variety of words or is there an over-repetition of key terms? If you have used a thesaurus to increase the vocabulary of the essay, have you checked in the OED, and possibly a dictionary of critical terms, that you are using words appropriately in this context? Here are three categories of words to avoid: slang, clichés, euphemisms.
- **Register** An essay on literature should be written with a degree of formality. This means that it should not contain anecdotes, slang, euphemisms or informal language. The language that you might use when chatting in a seminar or with friends is not usually appropriate for your written work. For example, there are many accounts of characters who experience mental-health problems in literature; it is not a good idea to refer to them as 'nutters', 'loonies', 'headcases', 'mentalists', etc. Attaining the right degree of formality can feel unnatural and can take a bit of practice; in

consequence, students often travel too far in the opposite direction and resort to archaisms or pomposity – as we'll see below there's no need to use terms like 'one', as in 'one might find', for example. Again, your reading will help you here; if you can read the successful essays of former students you can appropriate their style.

4.11.1 Proof-reading

You might feel that, if you've presented a brilliant argument with interesting evidence, a few typos and grammatical errors here and there won't matter, but these show a lack of care about your work and for your reader. They can also lead to some misunderstandings and unintentional humour (I once wrote an essay that included reference to Virginia Woolf's wok, not her work; an error that a spellchecker didn't pick up, and that probably ended up being the most memorable feature of the essay. Such errors have a tendency to stick in the reader's mind, unfortunately). In an ideal world someone else would proof-read your work for you. When you are reading your own words, it is very hard to stop yourself thinking about the content and not the surface errors. This is one reason why I have given editing and proof-reading their own sections in this book; to emphasise that one is about reading for content and one for mechanical mistakes. Again, the best strategy would be to swap essays with a friend and undertake each other's proofing. Here are some techniques and things to look out for, whether you are proofing your own or someone else's work.

Proof-reading techniques

Note The best tip for proof-reading is to read your script for one error at a time. Don't attempt to check all aspects of presentation, spelling, punctuation, etc. in one go. Devote a reading to each issue. You'll be far more likely to spot mistakes this way.

- **Print out your work** You should always proof-read from a paper copy. Although it's a good idea to use the computer spellchecker before you print, this will only identify non-existent words and not words that are spelt correctly but are misplaced. A print-out will allow you to read with more ease, to check the layout and also to employ one cunning proofer's tip: that is to read backwards. Some professionals swear by reading from back to front since this prevents the reading for content that can prevent you from recognising surface errors. It's also a good idea to have a blank sheet of paper underlining the line that you are checking as another method of focusing your eye.

- **Read when you are awake** It's crucial to undertake proof-reading when you are feeling alert. This is quite tedious work and unless you are fresh you'll let your mind drift and the mistakes will pass you by.
- **Know your work** When your essays are marked, it's likely that your tutor will identify frequent errors; you may already know that your use of the possessive apostrophe is a bit shaky, for example. Collate a list of mistakes that you commonly make and devote a reading of your essay to each of them.
- **Keep tools to hand** Make life easy for yourself. Keep a dictionary, grammar book, thesaurus, etc. on your desk. You'll be far more inclined to check areas of uncertainty if these resources are close to hand.
- **Mark each page with an error on it** If you are checking a long document like a dissertation, tick the top of each page that has mistakes on it so that you don't miss them or have to spend ages looking for them when you come to make the corrections.

Things to look out for

- **Reference system** Are you following the recommended (or compulsory) referencing system? Have you done so consistently throughout the essay and bibliography? Have all the texts that you've cited been included in your bibliography? And, conversely, are there still texts in the bibliography that you've cut from the main body of your essay during revisions? Are the page numbers in your references correct?
- **Word limit** Are you safely within it? In most universities you will be harshly punished for exceeding the word limit (losing 10 per cent of possible marks) although some allow a 10 per cent margin of error, which means that if you write 2,199 words for a 2,000-word essay you'll escape without penalty, but not if you write 2,201. Tutors read hundreds of essays in their career and get quite good at knowing what a 3,000-word essay looks like in terms of its size, so don't chance a rough estimate that may catch you out. In chapter 6: References we'll consider which quotations can be included in your word count and which can't.
- **Presentation** Is your essay double-spaced in an approved font and size? Does it have clear margins for your tutor to provide commentary in?
- **Spelling mistakes and typos** As mentioned above, you must not rely solely on a computer to check your spelling because it won't be able to identify homophones (words that sound the same but are spelt differently, like *there* and *their*, *allowed* and *aloud*).

- **Punctuation** The success of Lynne Truss's bestseller *Eats, Shoots and Leaves* is one demonstration of the 'zero tolerance' of punctuation errors that many people have. To these readers, the meaning of any text that includes the 'grocer's apostrophe' (the adding of an apostrophe to any plural) or confuses *it's* for *its* etc., will be utterly lost. Your tutor may become so preoccupied with correcting errors of the apostrophe, or other punctuation mark, that the rest of your essay, its argument, may be completely lost. Don't let this happen! Learn how to punctuate and let your reader concentrate on your readings, not the mechanical side of your writing.

4.12 Finally, a frequently asked question: 'Is it OK to use "I"?'

This must be one of the questions that I am asked most frequently by students. On the one hand, the focus on one small word compared to the enormous process involved in essay writing seems surprising but, on the other hand, it is clear that within this question are bound up all the contentious issues of identity, individuality and authorship that we have seen at the heart of the English degree. Unfortunately, this also means that if you ask two different tutors you may get two different answers, so here I will outline a strategy that incoporates the best policy from each perspective.

Students often get upset at the idea that they cannot use 'I' because they assume that this means they are being told not to express their own opinions. This is not the case. You are being asked to analyse and present critical views and this clearly involves a representation of your own perspective. However, constantly introducing these opinions with phrases like 'In my opinion', 'I think', 'I believe' is rather a waste of words since it is, firstly, rather a statement of the obvious and, secondly, it suggests a lack of confidence. If it wasn't your opinion or you didn't think it, you'd have introduced the argument with words like 'Woolf's essay suggests', and to flag up a statement with the disclaimer that it is what you think indicates a tentativeness, ironically a lack of belief. There are many occasions when it may be appropriate to write explicitly from a first-person perspective, however, particularly when you wish to differentiate your view from a critic's, with a phrase like 'Against Booth, I argue'.

Works cited

Truss, Lynne. *Eats, Shoots and Leaves*. London: Profile Books, 2003.

Womack, Peter. 'What Are Essays For?' *English in Education* 27.2 (Summer 1993): 42–9.

Jekyll and Hyde essay extracts

The actual marks awarded were 35 for the first one and 85 for the second.

Chapter 5

Sentences

If you pick up a selection of this week's newspapers, it won't take long before you come across an article decrying the standard of young people's written communication skills. Here's a startling, and yet typical, example from the *Guardian*: according to the UK Recruitment and Employment Commission, 'graduates are twice as likely to make mistakes as those who did not go to university' in their CVs and letters of application (Jones and Ashton). What kind of mistakes are they making? Mainly spelling errors or grammatical ones, apparently. What does that mean? The *OED* defines grammar as:

> that department of the study of a language which deals with its inflexional forms or other means of indicating the relations of words in the sentence, and with the rules for employing these in accordance with established usage; usually including also the department which deals with the phonetic system of the language and the principles of its representation in writing.

If only there was a Department, a physical place, where we could go to discover these rules and 'established usage' of English. Because the biggest difficulty of being requested to be precise in your use of language is that there is no universal or standardised guidebook to English grammar, with rules that everyone in English-speaking communities adheres to. Firstly, spoken and written grammars are different: what is acceptable in speech may not be in writing. Secondly, there are substantial differences between UK, US and other Englishes. Thirdly, even within these countries you will discover that there are variations in the 'established usage', the way that many forms are addressed, issues that some grammarians are strict about but that others regard as anachronisms, arguing that as times change, so does grammar. (One example is the 'split infinitive'; some assert that you should never insert an adverb between 'to' and the verb – as in 'to wildly gesticulate' – while others feel that this is a matter of style and so if you prefer 'to wildly gesticulate' to 'to gesticulate wildly' you should feel free to use it.) Fourthly, many users of the English language don't know the rules anyway, and so you'll find countless examples of grammatical errors in the newspapers, novels, letters, mail outs and flyers that you read on a daily basis. All this might make you want to throw up your hands in despair and call for the abolition of primers, the death of rules. And you might think, judging from these almost daily complaints in the media about the poor writing standards of young employees, that this is what most people have done.

As students of literature, of the written word, you might be expected to have a higher standard of written communication than your peers in other disciplines. Certainly, you are likely to find that your tutors lack tolerance of your grammatical errors. As I've stated earlier in this book, even minor mistakes that you don't notice or mind can loom large for your reader, preventing him or her from focusing on what you actually have to say. At the other end of the spectrum, you will gain low marks for essays that cannot be read because the words are hard to identify and the sentences incomplete. There is nothing more frustrating than receiving a graded essay from a tutor who has been lavish with the red ink of grammatical correction but has failed to engage with your ideas. This is the best reason for attempting some understanding of what the 'rules' of language are: to enhance the clarity of your communication. You want people to listen to and understand what you have to say, and you want them to be able to do so with ease. In every area of your life you want to be able to express yourself and be heard.

You'll notice that I have called this chapter not Grammar but Sentences. This is partly because the idea of grammar is so off-putting, and partly because the term is used quite loosely – and incorrectly – to cover all aspects of language, but mainly because even the field of language, to which it accurately refers, could not be covered in one small chapter of one small book. Let us consider what grammar does not refer to. It does not refer to style or register; these are matters of choice, taste and occasion, not accuracy. It does not refer to spelling or the mechanics of presentation that will be discussed in the next chapter. It does encompass syntax and thus, in its facility for indicating a correctly presented sentence, also punctuation. A brief discussion could not hope to cover sentences in their entirety but in titling the chapter thus, I want to suggest that it is about the smaller units of your written communication as a literature student. This chapter, then, is about more and less than grammar. In thinking about sentences, it will not provide a survey of the grammar of the English language and use the terminology of the linguist with reference to 'types of lexical auxiliary' and the like, but it will consider common errors and the ways that some stylistic choices can alter meaning. Understanding the stylistic implications of grammatical structures will clearly enhance your readings of literary texts, but my main focus here is with your own writing and with the mistakes that are most frequently found in student assignments.

Further reading

If you feel that your knowledge of the basics is weak, then you should look to some more comprehensive guides, of which there are many. You may already have a favourite or your tutor may recommend one but here is a small selection that demonstrates the range of materials on offer: *OWL*, the Online Writing Lab at Purdue is an excellent site with a search engine for grammar (and referencing systems) (http://owl.english.purdue.edu); David Crystal's *Rediscover Grammar* is concise, with accessible examples; Börjars and Burridge, *Introducing English Grammar*, is an introduction to the sentence structure of English with real examples from the English and Australian editions of the magazine for homeless people, *The Big Issue*; Stott and Chapman's *Grammar and Writing* is expressly designed for English students and employs literary texts as examples; Fowler's *Modern English Usage* is the guide to British English that many journalists still refer to, and Bryan Garner has written an American version; although Downing and Locke's *English Grammar* is designed for speakers of English as a second language, its clear layout and encyclopedic coverage will appeal to you if you are keen to have a thorough knowledge of grammatical structures. Karen Elizabeth Gordon has been lauded for managing to introduce a gothic sensuality to the instruction of grammar in her series of handbooks for 'the Innocent, the Eager and the Doomed'.

 If you are more concerned with issues of style, then Strunk and White's *The Elements of Style* is a 'dusty rule book' that has become an American classic; Williams, *Style: Ten Lessons in Clarity and Grace*, is a more recent text in the same vein; Trask, *Mind the Gaffe*, offers an alphabetical list of words and features that the 'careful writer' should avoid; although Kaplan, *Editing Made Easy*, is primarily designed to help journalists make their English 'clear, active, interesting' its affable tone and brevity make it an appealing desk companion for any student.

5.1 The most common errors made in student assignments

Here is a list of the twenty most common mistakes found in student assignments, according to a survey carried out by Connors and Lunsford (quoted in Gottschalk and Hjortshoj 97–8):

- No comma after an introductory element
- Vague pronoun reference
- No comma in compound sentence
- Wrong word
- No comma with non-restrictive element
- Wrong or missing inflected verb endings
- Wrong or missing preposition

- Comma splice
- Possessive apostrophe
- Tense shift
- Unnecessary shift in person (pronoun)
- Sentence fragment
- Wrong tense or verb form
- Subject–verb agreement
- Lack of comma in a series
- Pronoun agreement
- Unnecessary comma(s) with restrictive element
- Run-on or fused sentence
- Dangling or misplaced modifier
- Its/it's error

Response

How many of these terms do you recognise? Do you understand what the faults are? Do you know if you are guilty of any of them? Do you know how to correct them?

Through a discussion of these mistakes, I hope to provide at least an introduction to the elements of sentence construction that you will need to master, in order to write well. Rather than approach each error as it appears in this list, I have grouped them under headings that refer to their sentence element.

5.2 Errors involving clauses

What is a clause? Clauses are structural units. A sentence must be composed of one or more complete clauses. The smallest clause is one that consists of the **subject** and the **verb**, such as 'he ate', which could be a sentence on its own: 'He ate.' This is known as a **simple** sentence. But most simple sentences and clauses consist of more than this: 'he ate quickly' or 'he ate an apple', for example. The first example still has a **subject** and a **verb** unit ('quickly' adds meaning to the verb) and the second is a **subject**, **verb**, **object** structure, believed to be the most common structure of English clauses ('an apple' is the **object**).

If the clause was joined to at least one other then it would form a **multiple** sentence, for example, 'He ate an apple and drank a cup of tea.' There are two types of multiple sentence: **compound** and **complex**. The example I have just given is compound; this means that it is composed of two **independent** (also known as **main**) clauses that could stand alone as grammatically complete sentences, i.e. 'He ate an apple.' '[He] drank a cup of tea.' A complex sentence is composed of (at least) an independent clause and a **subordinate** clause, such as, 'He ate quickly because he was late for work.' Here, the independent clause is 'He ate quickly' – it could stand alone as a sentence – while the subordinate clause, 'because he was late for work' is dependent upon the rest of the sentence for sense and grammatical accuracy. Alone, 'because he was late for work' leaves us hanging, since there is information missing. (Note how the independent clause could precede or follow the subordinate clause to still make sense and complete the sentence: 'Because he was late for work, he ate quickly.')

The problem is that although my examples are straightforward, most sentences are not. Consider the sentences that I have written in this book, for example. In order to ensure that you have written a grammatically complete and accurately punctuated sentence, you need to work out its different clauses. This can be incredibly difficult and is often not the science you might hope and expect it to be, but a matter of intuition because there are many other possible sentence components; it is not always easy to identify to which clause the extra details belong. However, a clause will always have at least a subject and a verb; if it doesn't have these then it is a different structural unit. For example, in the sentence 'He ate an apple, a sandwich and a tub of ice-cream', 'a tub of ice-cream', lacking a verb, is part of the object rather than a new clause.

Co-ordinators and conjunctions

In sentences that have more than one clause, one way to identify which are independent and which are subordinate is to look for the words or punctuation mark that joins them together. We will consider the punctuation possibilities below and think about the words that connect clauses here. Independent clauses are joined by *co-ordinators* while *conjunctions* are the words that join subordinate clauses to independent ones. While there are only three co-ordinators – **and**, **or**, **but** – there are many conjunctions. In terms of function, they can be largely divided into two groups: those that relate to time (such as **before**, **since**, **when**) and those that relate to contingency (including **if**, **unless**, **although**). In terms of appearance, these examples are all *simple* conjunctions because they consist of only one word; there are also *conjunctive groups*, which include phrases like **soon after**, **even though**, **in order to** and **as if**.

A list of some conjunctions

When, where, whenever, after, before, since, while, whilst, until, if, unless, as, provided that, except that, so, so that, in order that, for, unlike, because.
Note If you see one of these words or phrases, then your sentence contains a subordinate clause.

5.2.1 Presenting only a fragment of a sentence

Being encouraged to analyse your work for identifiable clauses can lead to over-zealous punctuation. The most common fragments occur when writers think every clause or structural unit is a sentence. Here is an example: 'Irving's early work such as "Rip Van Winkle" was taken directly from the stories of Peter Klaus. Which appeared in Otmar's collection of tales.' The first sentence is grammatically complete, but the second is a subordinate clause (introduced by the conjunction 'which') that should be joined to it with a comma instead. It's worth noting, however, that sentence fragments can be used appropriately in other arenas: think of the question-and-answer format in journalists' interviews, or in jokes, for example.

> **Note** Remember every sentence must have at least one independent clause.

5.2.2 Presenting fused or run-on sentences

This mistake is the opposite of the one above. Instead of effectively combining clauses through co-ordination or subordination, a series of sentences is presented as one. How could you break down the following run-on sentence? 'To be an American writer in this era was extremely forbidding there was a lack of respect of American writers by European critics Americans did not regard writing as a legitimate profession.' One way to do it would be to give each independent clause its own sentence: 'To be an American writer in this era was extremely forbidding. There was a lack of respect of American writers by European critics. Americans did not regard writing as a legitimate profession.' However, this is rather jerky to read and it fails to present a causal connection between the issues. A better alternative might be: 'To be an American writer in this era was extremely forbidding, since there was a lack of respect of American writers by European critics and Americans did not regard writing as a legitimate profession.' Here we have two independent clauses – 'To be an American writer in this era was extremely forbidding' 'Americans did not regard writing as a legitimate profession' – but we have made a causal relationship through the subordination of the clause 'since there was a lack of respect of American writers by European critics'.

5.2.3 The dangling or misplaced modifier

'Having examined *America is in the Heart* for the quest for identity, Carlos Bulosan struggled to fit into American society.' Can you tell what is wrong

> **Response to 5.2.2**
>
> - Can you see how the meaning has been subtly inflected by the alternative punctuation? How else might the sentence be punctuated? And how would this give a different emphasis to or relationship between the elements?
> - Take a look at a recent essay of your own. Starting with just one page, see if you can firstly, identify whether or not your sentences are grammatically complete, and secondly, whether alternative methods of joining clauses would inflect the meaning differently. Can you see ways to improve your sentence structure?

with this sentence? The grammatical confusion contained here relates to the subject of each clause. The second clause is the independent clause; it could stand alone as a sentence: 'Carlos Bulosan struggled to fit into American society.' In the first clause, it seems that the writer, the student, has examined the text; the student is the **implied subject**, but in the second clause Carlos Bulosan, who wrote the autobiography *America is in the Heart*, is the **explicit subject**. Can you see that they don't match? The first clause is what is known as the 'dangling' or 'misplaced' modifier or participle: it dangles because it isn't clearly attached to the subject in the sentence's independent clause. This sentence isn't great but in order to make it at least grammatically correct and a little clearer to understand it should read: 'Having examined *America is in the Heart* for the quest for identity, I found that Carlos Bulosan struggled to fit into American society.' Now we know who has examined the text.

5.3 Errors involving commas

In comparison with the perceived complexities of the colon and semi-colon, the comma seems like a friendly little punctuation mark that you might want to rely on when a punctuation mark is called for. In fact, the simplicity of its appearance belies a set of rules with more variations and possible confusions than the designated purpose of other marks. When I was a student myself, I was given the enormously misleading advice that commas were like breathing spaces and should be inserted into sentences at the point where you would take a pause if you were reading them out loud. This is not helpful advice and following it did not lead to the accurate punctuation of my essays.

5.3.1 The comma splice

This is an error where a comma is used instead of a full stop (period in the US), semi-colon or co-ordinator. It can happen when writers haven't correctly identified whether clauses are independent or subordinate. The comma splice is the name given to the mistaken use of a comma to join two independent clauses in a sentence without a co-ordinator. Here is an example: 'Modernism is a term that is used to describe a literary era, it is sometimes known as the age of anxiety.' The three correct ways to join independent clauses are:

- **full stop/period**
  'Modernism is a term that is used to describe a literary era. It is sometimes known as the age of anxiety.'
- **semi-colon**
  'Modernism is a term that is used to describe a literary era; it is sometimes known as the age of anxiety.'
- **co-ordinator**
  'Modernism is a term that is used to describe a literary era and it is some-times known as the age of anxiety.'

Alternatively, you could make one of the clauses subordinate and use a conjunction to connect them, for example: '**Although** modernism is a term that is used to describe a literary era, it is sometimes known as the age of anxiety.'

Response

What are the stylistic and interpretive implications of the alternatives to the incorrect sentence? See if there are examples of the comma splice in your own writing and correct them in any manner that you find meaningful and elegant.

5.3.2 The absence of a comma after an introductory element

An introductory element in a sentence could be a phrase or an individual word. It is important to segregate it from the rest of the sentence by a comma, so that your independent clause is clear for your reader to see. Examples of the many possible one-word introductions are 'Finally', 'Indeed', 'Instead', and adjectives such as 'Overjoyed, she . . .' Likewise, there are countless possible introductory elements; they include subordinate clauses, such as 'Although Woolf is known as a feminist, critics argue that . . .', or prepositional phrases like 'At first' or 'During that time'. Commas should not be used to break off the beginning of any element that forms part of the subject or verb phrase, though.

5.3.3 The absence of a comma in a compound sentence

This is a rule that some people dispute, claiming instead that it is a matter of stylistic choice, especially if the clauses are short and the sentence unambiguous. Meanwhile, advocates argue that a comma should be placed in a compound sentence before the co-ordinator, for example: 'Woolf claimed to be a feminist, but some critics disagree.' There is a general trend towards minimal use of punctuation, and so it's likely that this is one rule that may not continue to be stringently observed.

5.3.4 The absence of a comma with a non-restrictive element

A non-restrictive element, also known as a non-defining relative clause, is a piece of information that is added parenthetically; it could be omitted from the sentence and the sentence would still make sense. The non-restrictive element is most commonly indicated by its setting within two commas, but brackets or dashes can also be used. In the sentence 'Shakespeare, who is considered by many to be the greatest ever playwright, was born in 1564', the non-restrictive clause could be omitted for the sentence to remain grammatically correct and meaningful as 'Shakespeare was born in 1564.' The mistake that is commonly made is the omission of the second comma, for example: 'Shakespeare, who is considered by many to be the greatest ever playwright was born in 1564.' The example I have given is a straightforward one; in other more ambiguous cases, the use or lack of commas to indicate whether the element is non-restrictive or restrictive can significantly alter the sentence's meaning.

5.3.5 Unnecessary comma(s) with a restrictive element

A restrictive element, or defining clause, as you might guess from the definition of its opposite above, is a piece of information that is crucial to the meaning of a sentence. The mistake of marking it out with commas would signal its status as additional rather than essential information, leading to confusion and inaccuracy. Consider the different meanings implied in the two versions of this sentence: 'The two students, who were found guilty of plagiarism, failed the course.' / 'The two students who were found guilty of plagiarism failed the course.' In the first version, the fact that the students were guilty of plagiarism is not signalled as the reason for their failure. This is presented as additional information and as such may be just a coincidence. In the second version, the plagiarism is presented as a restrictive element: it is crucial information and thus indicates that it is the reason why the students failed the course. Both sentences are grammatically correct but the different deployment of commas presents different meanings.

Using commas around what is a restrictive element will perplex your reader. In the sentence 'In *Song of Solomon*, Morrison's character, Guitar, is consumed with greed for gold', the name of the protagonist has been placed within commas signalling that it is a non-restrictive element. This would be fine if there was only one character in *Song of Solomon*, but as there are several key figures the name of Guitar is crucial information and thus is a restrictive element that should not be contained within commas.

5.3.6 The absence of a comma in a series

Also known as the serial comma, the Oxford comma and the Harvard comma, this is another issue about which there is, if not dispute, regional variation. In the US, it is the rule to place a comma before the last item in a list, as in: 'Critics who have influenced the study of cinema include Deleuze and Guattari, Laura Mulvey, Stephen Heath, and Teresa de Lauretis.' Traditionally, in the UK this list would be presented without the comma after 'Heath'. (Notice that I didn't include one after 'Oxford comma' in the list in the first sentence of this paragraph.) I actually find the US use of this comma very helpful because it clarifies each element of the list precisely. Gilles Deleuze and Félix Guattari co-authored several texts and count as one item on the list above; in the UK formula, this would look very confusing if it had been differently sequenced, for example: 'Critics who have influenced the study of cinema include Laura Mulvey, Stephen Heath, Deleuze and Guattari and Teresa de Lauretis.' The American mode would look much better: 'Critics who have influenced the study of cinema include Laura Mulvey, Stephen Heath, Deleuze and Guattari, and Teresa de Lauretis.' In this version, it is clearly signalled that Deleuze and Guattari wrote together and not individually, which is informative for the reader who has not heard of them.

5.4 Errors involving apostrophes

The misuse of apostrophes is a source of enormous irritation to many people. It's hard to know why errors involving this punctuation mark cause more aggravation than others; some cynics suggest that it is simply because rules involving possessive apostrophes are easier to follow and more widely known than those governing colons and semi-colons, etc. Alternatively, it may be the scale upon which this grammatical crime is committed. Walk down a street and you are likely to be confronted with the mistake in shop names and signs. Indeed, one error has become known as 'the grocer's apostrophe' in recognition of the frequency with which these traders advertise **apple's** or **tomato's** for sale. The mistaken assumption of the greengrocer is that an apostrophe is added to a noun with an 's' when the noun becomes plural. This is not the case.

5.4.1 The misuse of the possessive apostrophe

So when is it appropriate to use the possessive apostrophe? The answer is in the name: it denotes not plurality as the greengrocer thinks but possession. So, the play written by Caryl Churchill becomes not **Churchills *A Number*** but **Churchill's *A Number***; the course on drama by women is not **Womens Drama** but **Women's Drama**; the problems experienced by one family become not the **families problems** but the **family's problems**; and you go to the library to borrow **DVDs** not **DVD's**.

It may be that you find adding a possessive apostrophe to a singular noun is straightforward but the problem arises when the noun is plural. Remember, if you are indicating collective ownership, the apostrophe comes after the 's', but before the 's' if the owner is singular. So, if you were discussing the rules of one school you'd write **the school's rules** but if you were talking about school rules generally, you'd write **schools' rules**; **the student's exam** would refer to the examination of one particular student, while **the students' exam** indicates the exam taken by a group of them. Problems occur when faced with words that change in the plural, for instance, families and universities. The change in spelling from 'y' to 'ies' already denotes plurality; to show possession you add an apostrophe after the 'ies', for example, **the universities' expansion scheme** refers to the expansion of the whole sector, while **the university's expansion scheme** indicates the growth of an individual university; **the universities expansion scheme** is grammatically inaccurate and as such does not indicate anything.

> **Note** When checking if you've correctly inserted a possessive apostrophe, you can turn the phrase around and see if it makes sense. So, for example, 'Dickens's novels' can be 'the novels of Dickens' and still retain its meaning.

Other common apostrophe errors

- **Decades** A very common mistake is to record time periods as, for example, **the 1960's**. This is wrong; it should be recorded as **the 1960s**. All of the following examples are accurate:

- In the 1890s, the developing feminist outlook became known as the New Woman movement.
- The 1890s' New Woman movement was feminist.
- The New Woman movement of the nineties was feminist.
- The nineties' New Woman movement was feminist.

- **Plurals that don't end in 's'** There are some noun plurals that don't end in 's'; instead, a change to the spelling of the singular already indicates plurality. The main ones are **people** (from the singular 'person'), **children** (from child), **men** (from man) and **women** (from woman). In these cases, you add apostrophe 's' as with single nouns, for example, **the children's mother** and **the people's princess**. Note that while **womens' clothes** is incorrect, there is an accurate use of **peoples' beliefs** in which the plural peoples are the peoples of the world, understood to have different experiences of humanity, not a small homogenous group of people.
- **Words that already end in 's'** Nouns that already end in 's' can cause confusion. To say **Jesus's disciples** is a mouthful and so it is becoming acceptable for such words to be written as **Jesus' disciples**, for example. This can apply to any nouns that already end in 's' but it is mainly ones with the 'zuz' sound at the end that cause the problem. A case like **the princess's tiara**, for instance, is not so hard to enunciate.

5.4.2 Confusion between its and it's

An exception to the rule of inserting an apostrophe to denote possession is with the word **its**. This little word already indicates ownership. For example, in the sentence 'The cat sat on its mat', the mat belongs to the cat, it is the cat's mat. The word **it's** is an abbreviation of **it is** and thus its use in the sentence 'The cat sat on it's mat' is mistaken because this would mean 'The cat sat on it is mat', which doesn't make sense. **Its** belongs to the group of words known as possessive pronouns, which all contain ownership in their meaning. They are **mine, yours, his, hers, its, ours** and **theirs**. None of these words needs a possessive apostrophe. The 's' at the end of the words **yours, ours** and **theirs** already indicates possession; your's, our's, their's are wrong.

Common contractions that should always have apostrophes to indicate missing letters include: I'm (I am), he's (he is), they're (they are), we're (we are), haven't (have not), won't (will not), can't (cannot), couldn't (could not), doesn't (does not), didn't (did not), isn't (is not) and, of course, it's (it is). Some tutors feel that such abbreviations have no place in formal essays, so if you do want to use them please ensure that the apostrophe is accurately located.

> **Note** An apostrophe indicates one of two things: possession or contraction. Whenever you attempt to insert one, ask yourself, 'Am I using this apostrophe to indicate that there is an element of a word missing or to indicate ownership?' If the answer is 'no' then the apostrophe isn't necessary.

Two last words about punctuation

- **The hyphen** This mark is used to connect words or parts of words that belong together. The error I wish to highlight here is the incorrect use of the hyphen to join two words together that should be left to stand alone. Hyphens are used to connect adjectival phrases and compound adjectives. (Adjectives are words that are used to modify nouns.) So, when referring to the twentieth century as a noun, the two words should not be hyphenated, but when using them as an adjectival phrase to add information to another noun, they should be hyphenated, as in 'twentieth-century literature'.

> **Note** Adjectival phrases containing adverbs ending in –ly are not hyphenated, for example, 'a hurriedly finished task' rather than a 'hurriedly-finished task'.

- **The colon** What are colons for?
  - They are used to introduce long quotations (as we'll see in the next chapter).
  - They are used to introduce a list.
  - They are used to show that what follows is an amplification of what has been said in the first part of the sentence. Imagine inserting the phrase 'that is to say' in place of the colon and if this works then your colon use is accurate.

> **Note** In the UK at least it is not correct to capitalise the first letter after a colon as though it were a new sentence, although I have noticed several instances of this in recent publications.

5.5 Errors involving pronouns

Pronouns, sharing some grammatical features with nouns, are the words that stand in for nouns (or noun phrases) for the sake of brevity and in order to avoid linguistic repetition. The most common sub-class is the group of **personal pronouns**:

Subject	I	we	you (single)	you (plural)	he	she	it	they
Object	me	us	you	you	him	her	it	them

But they also include **possessive pronouns** that we've seen above (mine, yours, etc.), **reflexive pronouns** such as himself, myself and yourself, and **indefinite pronouns** ending in 'thing' or 'body' such as something, anything, anybody and everyone.

5.5.1 Vague pronoun reference

The virtue of pronouns is their very generalised reference or widespread application but this can also cause ambiguity for your reader. To avoid tedious repetition, you substitute pronouns like 'his' and 'he' for the proper noun, the specific name of an author, such as Joseph Conrad, for example. Sometimes, it is not clear to whom the 'he' or 'his' refers. Consider the following example: 'In a letter to his collaborator, Ford Madox Ford, Conrad told him that his theories of literary Impressionism would be influential.' Whose literary Impressionism will be influential: Ford's or Conrad's? This is an error that can particularly arise after editing, when sentences have been shifted around and the name that preceded a pronoun may no longer be there.

5.5.2 Lack of agreement between pronouns

In a bid to avoid the gendered connotation of using 'he' to refer to any unnamed singular person, the word 'they', which is plural, is frequently used instead without people realising that it is an error. For example, you might be surprised to discover that the following sentence is grammatically incorrect: 'Anyone can write a good essay if they work hard enough.' It should be: 'Anyone can write a good essay if he works hard enough' or 'Anyone can write a good essay if she or he works hard enough.' One way to avoid both the gender bias and unacceptable usage is to convert the subject of the sentence to a plural. So, for instance, instead of 'From the opening chapter, **the reader** is made aware that **he** will enter the mind of a disturbed individual', the subject could be changed to 'readers': 'From the opening chapter, **readers** are made aware that they will enter the mind of a disturbed individual'; but 'From the opening chapter, **the reader** is made aware that **they** will enter the mind of a disturbed individual' is incorrect.

5.5.3 *Unnecessary shift in person (pronoun)*

This error, like the one above, occurs when the agent of the sentence, its subject, changes. An example is 'Reading *Jane Eyre* in the twenty-first century, **I** find **you** have great sympathy for Bertha Mason', where the subject has switched from the first person to the second when it should remain stable. In English, there are three persons: the first (speaker/s or writers: **I**); the second (the person/s addressed: **you**); the third (any persons who are not the speaker/s, writer/s or addressees: **he, she, they**, named people or groups, for example). The third person includes non-personal entities; **it** is often a word that is empty of meaning, for example: '**It**'s hard to know why he did that', or has very generalised meanings, for example, about life: 'How's **it** going?' or the weather, 'What's **it** like outside?'

5.6 Errors involving verbs

You might have been told that verbs are 'doing' words but this definition, although a helpful aide-mémoire, is slightly misleading since as many verbs denote processes and states as actions or events. For example, in the sentence 'She suffers from depression', the verb 'to suffer' describes an ongoing experience rather than an activity or action. In the statement 'He is forty-five', the word 'is', the third-person singular of the verb 'to be', also describes a state of being rather than something that is consciously carried out. Identifying verbs, as you have already gathered from our discussion of clauses and sentence structure above, is crucial to writing clearly and accurately. The reason for this is that in English verbs are the class of words subject to the most **inflectional** variety and complexity. Inflection (remember this word in the *OED*'s definition of grammar?) refers to the way the form of a word is changed to match the person, number and tense of the subject or object that it is paired with.

There are three types of verb: **full** (also known as **main** or **lexical**), **modal auxiliary** and **primary**.

- **Full** verbs are those that contain meaning, for example, 'write', 'enjoy', 'perform', 'understand'. These verbs, given here in their base forms (as they would appear in a dictionary), are inflected to fit the subject or object they are attached to. This category of verbs is enormous, expanding and unlimited.
- There are nine **modal auxiliary** verbs: can, could, may, might, shall, should, will, would and must. These verbs express a variety of judgements about probability or obligation of events. They function as auxiliaries in that they

Gender and language

In English, nouns are subject to very little inflection; most often they are inflected to indicate number, for example, 'book' is modified to 'books' once a word indicating plurality (for example, 'some', 'seven') is placed before it. In Romance languages – descendants of Latin: Spanish, Portuguese, French, Italian and Romanian – nouns are inflected to denote gender, for example, in French a female friend is 'amie', a male one 'ami', but there are very few nouns like this in English. Even occupations with titles indicating gender are going out of fashion. In a guide to Grantchester, the small village outside Cambridge beloved of many literary figures, Sylvia Plath is referred to as a 'poetess' rather than a poet. This is not an acceptable designation to use in an essay.

are added to the full verb to refine its meaning and have some unique grammatical properties.

- Modals have only one form. Even when the subject of the sentence changes, the modal does not. For example, 'I *might* go to the cinema', 'He *might* go to the cinema', 'We *might* have gone to the cinema, if it had been open.'
- The first verb that follows a modal must appear in the base infinitive form. In the first two examples above, the verb 'to go' remains in its base form despite the fact that without the modal it would be inflected as 'I go' and 'He goes.'

● There are three **primary** verbs: **be**, **have** and **do**. They can function either as main verbs on their own, or as auxiliaries attached to full verbs. Here are some examples:
- As main verbs: 'Conrad **was** Polish, but he **had** success as a writer in English.'
- As auxiliary verbs: 'He **is** going to the library', 'They **have** finished the wine', 'I **don't** [**do** not] understand.' The use of primary verbs as auxiliaries gives information about when the event took place or will take place.

There is one other way of classifying verbs: as **finite** or **non-finite**. The **finite** forms of verbs are those that have changed to indicate number, person, tense or mood. The first verb in a verb phrase is always finite: for example, 'He **was** going to read the novel', 'They **hadn't** achieved the results they wanted.' Here are examples of the other ways that finite verbs change:

● Finite verbs showing a contrast in number and person: 'I **read**', 'She **reads**', 'He **is**', 'You **are**.'
● Finite verbs showing a contrast in tense: 'They **live** in Brighton. They **lived** in New York.'

- Finite verbs showing a contrast in mood. There are three broad types of finite verb phrases that indicate mood: **indicative**, **subjunctive** and **imperative**.
    - The most common type of verb phrase is **indicative**; it is used to state or question factual matters, for example, '**I'm** cross.' '**Is it** raining?'
    - The **subjunctive** expresses wishes, conditions and other non-factual situations, for example, 'I demanded that Tony **apologise**.' Note, if the sentence was indicative (indicating a factual statement: that Tony had apologised), the verb apologise would be inflected: 'I demanded that Tony **apologised**.'
    - The **imperative** is used for directive statements, for example, '**Go** away. **Leave** me alone.'

Non-finite forms don't vary in this way and therefore don't express contrasts in number, person, tense or mood. There are three non-finite forms of the verb:

- The –ing participle: For example, '**Walking** down the road, I met my friends' does not change even when I switch around the subject to '**Walking** down the road, my friends met me.'
- The –ed participle: In this example, '**Bored**, she gave an audible sigh' the non-finite **bored** doesn't change however the subject changes, thus the sentence, '**Bored** by the long discussion, the whole seminar group was restless.'
- The base form used as an **infinitive**: 'to read', 'to write', 'to dream'. For example, 'I used to like **to read** and my parents still like **to read**.'

5.6.1 Unnecessary shift in tense

Can you see what has happened in this extract from a student essay?

> The Contagious Diseases Act (1864) was set up because of the overwhelming public concern about venereal disease that was mainly associated with the idea that the prostitutes 'carried' diseases. The act enforced on the idea that if a woman is believed to be committing prostitution by an officer of the law then she can be forcefully searched in order to provide evidence, if she is suffering from venereal disease, she could be detained in a hospital for a period of up to three months.

It starts, rightly, in the past, about an Act that *was* set up, but moves into the present, discussing the idea that women *can* be searched (the past of *can* is *could*). Sometimes this error is committed within one sentence. Although journalists often tell stories in the present tense to vivify them, before moving on to a discussion of past events in the past tense, your essays should not meander through time. Some tutors feel that, especially if you are writing about the past, the only appropriate tenses for such assignments are past tenses. If you are discussing a general principle or the work of contemporary writers and critics, you might feel it is appropriate to write in the present; however, the fact that you are discussing recorded words might negate this. Whatever your feeling, ensure that you write in the tense you intend, and that you do not vary it within a single sentence.

5.6.2 Wrong tense or verb form

The appearance and explanation of these errors cannot be generally diagnosed since they are inevitably wide-ranging and each case is particular. Furthermore, what is an error in standard British and American usage may well be an acceptable form in different regional variations. Here is one example that I encounter regularly, being asked, 'What was your address?' when the speaker is requesting not a former address but the one of my current residence, and thus the question should be, 'What *is* your address?' Confusion about the tense and exact meanings of the modal auxiliary verbs causes their widespread misuse in a similar way. Again, when making holiday plans I am asked by the agent who wants to know my dates of travel, 'When would you be going?' instead of, 'When *are* you going?' The verb 'would' implies a contingency that is inaccurate since I have already booked my time off work and I know I will be going away then. If there was a degree of uncertainty about my trip, the correct question would be, 'When *will* you be going to Tenerife, if you get the time off work?' and the modal 'would' is only correct in this scenario: 'When would you have gone, if you had been able to get the time off work?' However, while this usage is unacceptable in standard forms of British and American English, it is acceptable in some regional variations.

Response

Look carefully at examples of your own writing to see if you can identify any errors of tense in your verb use. Do you know how to use modal auxiliary verbs?

5.6.3 Wrong or missing inflected verb endings

Do you know how to inflect verbs? Correct the errors in these sentences:

- 'He study in the library.'
- 'Darwin use to write in a shed in his garden.'

The first sentence is not inflected to the person; it should be 'He stud**ies**.' The second is not inflected to the tense; it should be 'Darwin us**ed** to write' as he is long dead and the activity of his writing is over.

5.6.4 Lack of subject–verb agreement

Writing a long or complex sentence can sometimes result in this mistake, as you lose track of its subject. Remember that the verb phrase should always be attached and inflected according to a subject or object. Here's an example of a sentence that hasn't matched the verb to the subject: 'Alternatively, other characters such as Etta Mae Johnson also recognise that racism affects their daily lives and seeks to overcome it in smaller ways.' The verb 'seeks' has been inflected to match the singular person of Etta Mae Johnson and not the group of other characters in which she is included. It should therefore be 'seek'.

Passive and active sentences

In rules for good writing, exponents of clear English (including the Plain English Campaign www.plainenglish.co.uk/) always warn against using the passive sentence construction. The difference between passive and active sentences is whether or not the subject *acts* or *is acted upon*. In an active sentence the subject acts (is the agent) while in a passive sentence the subject is the recipient of action. Here is an example of the same information presented in both forms:

- **Active** Jacques Derrida and Paul de Man developed the textual practice known as Deconstruction.
- **Passive** The textual practice known as Deconstruction was developed by Jacques Derrida and Paul de Man.

In the active construction, Derrida and de Man are the subject and thus the focus of the sentence, while in the passive version, Deconstruction is the subject and focus. Choosing to write actively or passively is a way of giving different emphasis to the same information. Often passive constructions are used when the agent cannot be identified. So, for example, the sentence 'My jewellery was stolen', in which 'My jewellery' is the subject, implies that the thieves are unknown. This lack of an agent provides the reason why tutors encourage students not to employ the passive formula where possible, despite the fact that passive sentences have such valid uses. The overuse of passive sentences indicates a lack of confidence in what you have to say. Consider the following introduction:

> In this essay it will be shown that the representations of colonials and natives in Bacon's *New Atlantis* and Neville's *The Isle of Pines* can be contrasted. It can be seen that these utopias discuss issues relating to sexual practices and the treatment of racially different characters. It will

> be shown that the main purpose of utopic writing is to exhibit a society distinct from reality to draw attention to problems in it. It has been argued that utopias are a form of social criticism.

This passage has a repetitive structure that is monotonous and uninspiring. The author has completely removed the agent from every sentence giving the feeling that no one is responsible for the views promoted and that the essay has somehow formed itself out of thin air. This suggests a lack of confidence on the part of the author, as well as a lack of familiarity with critical sources. Even if you feel unwilling to commit your views to paper, you can attach opinions to critics as a way of making sentences active.

Passive sentences can be long and clumsy. Even the first, very simple example above is two words longer than the active version and this is an important consideration when writing essays to a strict word length. Passive sentences do have a place in our writing, as, for example, when the agent is unknown or the focus is upon the object and not the subject, but they must be deliberately and thoughtfully employed.

Response

How would you redraft the quoted passage on utopias to remove the passive sentence structures? It might help you to know that J. C. Davis is the author of a book on utopias from which the author has drawn some information.

Look again at examples of your own writing: do you use the passive structure frequently? Would your work be improved if more agents were identified?

5.7 Errors involving words

To avoid these errors, you must become friends with a dictionary, as I have constantly urged throughout this book. Attempting lexical variety through dependence on a thesaurus can cause the mistaken use of words, but as a glance at R. L. Trask's guide *Mind the Gaffe* reveals, many words are just generally misused. Trask's book takes the form of a dictionary but is a surprisingly interesting and enlightening read in itself.

5.7.1 Using the wrong word

The only way to ensure that this problem does not occur regularly in your work is the consistent reference to the dictionary to check even those words you think you know. Here are just a few examples of the many commonly misused words:

- **Advise/advice Advise** is a verb and **advice** is a noun. You can thus give someone some 'advice' or 'advise them', but you can't 'advice them'.
- **Affect/effect** Both can be a verb or a noun, but in either case **affect** refers to the emotional reaction produced by something, whereas effect refers to an automatic or general outcome of an action.
- **Dependant/dependent** A **dependant** is a noun; someone who depends upon someone else. In US English **dependent** can also be used to mean this, but in UK English the word **dependent** is an adjective that means 'depending on'. To write 'Interpretation is dependant upon your point of view' is therefore incorrect.
- **Disinterested** and **uninterested** These are not synonyms. If you are **disinterested** in something, you have no vested interest in it (you will not personally profit from it) while to be **uninterested** means that you have no interest in it. This means that you can be both disinterested in something and interested in it.
- **Fewer and less** Nouns can be classified as count or non-count. As their name indicates, count nouns are those that can be counted because they are interpreted as individuated entities, for example, 'book', 'friend'. In the singular they can be prefaced by the indefinite article 'a', 'an', but they can also be pluralised and occur with cardinal numbers, for example, 'an orange', 'seven essays'. Non-count (or mass) nouns are perceived as indivisible, uncountable masses of material like flour or, strangely, money. Grammatically they are treated as singular with 'some' and can't be used with words like 'many', 'those', 'thirteen', but many non-count nouns are matched with countable expressions such as 'a grain of flour' or 'a load of money'.

  Fewer and less have the same meaning in a sentence but in order to use the correct one you need to identify the noun you are attaching it to as either count or non-count. **Fewer** is used for count nouns (numbers); **less** is for non-count nouns (quantities).
  - There were **fewer** students at the seminar than last week. (**students** are countable)
  - He earns **less** money than she does. (**money** is non-countable)
  - She has **less** hope since she heard the news. (**hope** is non-countable)

Note There are some nouns that can be either count or non-count. Consider the change of meaning of the word 'beer' in the following questions:

- 'Would you like a beer?' (count)
- 'Do you like beer?' (non-count)

- **Infamous** This word is not a synonym for famous or notorious. It means 'notoriously wicked or bad', having achieved fame for wrongdoing.
- **Practise/practice Practise** is a verb and **practice** is a noun. You 'practise the violin' and discuss the 'religious practices of Western Buddhists'.
- **Which and that** Remember restrictive and non-restrictive clauses above? **That** introduces a restrictive clause and **which** introduces a non-restrictive one. Therefore, a clause beginning with 'which' should always be introduced by a comma and end with either another comma or a full stop. So, 'the book, which I wrote last year, has been published' is correct, as is 'the book that I wrote last year has been published', but 'the book which I wrote last year has been published' is not. This is another very common error that you will find repeated in many texts. It is therefore better to learn the rule and work out clauses rather than to look to existing prose for a model.

5.7.2 Using the wrong preposition or omitting a preposition

Prepositions belong to what is known as the minor class of words. There are two main categories of English words: major and minor. The major classes – nouns, verbs, adjectives and adverbs – are large, as their name suggests, and open; they are constantly changing and expanding to meet the new vocabulary needs of an evolving society. The major classes are deemed **lexical** because these words contain meaning instead of simply performing a structural function. In contrast, the minor classes – prepositions, conjunctions, determiners – are closed. Because they consist of words that assist the grammatical structures of language rather than its meaning, the content of these classes is fairly static. (This will be clear if you contrast the nouns **love, apathy** and **Zanzibar** with the prepositions **at, on** and **in**, for example.)

Prepositions are the words that express a relationship of space or time. They can be simple (one word) or complex (more than one word). Simple prepositions include: in, at, on, to, from, inside, with, of, off, into, after, before, behind. Complex prepositions include 'in addition to', 'because of', 'due to', 'except for', 'apart from'.

- **Within** During the past couple of years, I have noticed that this word is being used, with alarming frequency, in place of the smaller and correct preposition 'in'. 'Within' means inside, in an interior, an inner part; it is not a synonym for 'in' and so a phrase like 'within this essay' is incorrect. I've seen some horrible phrases like 'within a film environment' which could be replaced by the much more elegant, as well as accurate, 'in film' or 'in cinema'.

Works cited

Börjars, Kersti and Kate Burridge. *Introducing English Grammar*. London: Arnold, 2001.

Connors, Robert J. and Andrea A. Lunsford in 'Frequency of Formal Errors in Current College Writing, or Ma and Pa Kettle Do Research.' *College Composition and Communication* 39 (1988): 395–409.

Crystal, David. *Rediscover Grammar with David Crystal*. Revised edition. Harlow: Longman, 1997.

Davis, J. C. *Utopia and the Ideal Society: A Study of English Utopian Writing, 1516–1700*. Cambridge: Cambridge University Press, 1981.

Downing, Angela and Philip Locke. *English Grammar: A University Course*. 2nd ed. Abingdon, Oxon.: Routledge, 2006.

Fowler, H. W. *The New Fowler's Modern English Usage*. Rev. 3rd ed. Oxford: Oxford University Press, 1998.

Garner, Bryan. *Garner's American Usage*. Oxford: Oxford University Press, 2003.

Gordon, Karen Elizabeth. *The Deluxe Transitive Vampire: A Handbook of Grammar for the Innocent, the Eager and the Doomed*. Rev. ed. New York: Pantheon Books, 1993.

Gordon, Karen Elizabeth. *The New Well-Tempered Sentence: A Punctuation Handbook for the Innocent, the Eager and the Doomed*. Boston: Mariner Books, 2003.

Gottschalk, Katherine and Keith Hjortshoj. *The Elements of Teaching Writing: A Resource for Instructors in All Disciplines*. Boston and New York: Bedford/St Martin's, 2004.

Jones, Emma-Jayne and Robert Ashton. 'Bad Education.' *Guardian* 2 June 2007. Work: 1.

Kaplan, Bruce. *Editing Made Easy*. Camberwell, Victoria: Penguin, 2003.

OWL. The Online Writing Lab at Purdue. http://owl.english.purdue.edu

Stott, Rebecca and Peter Chapman, eds. *Grammar and Writing*. Speak–Write Series. Harlow: Pearson Education, 2001.

Strunk, William Jr and E. B. White. *The Elements of Style*. 4th ed. New York: Longman, 2000.

Trask, R. L. *Mind the Gaffe: The Penguin Guide to Common Errors in English*. London: Penguin, 2000.

Williams, Joseph M. *Style: Ten Lessons in Clarity and Grace*. 7th ed. New York: Longman, 2002.

Chapter 6

References

Everyone agrees on the importance of citing your references, but unfortunately there isn't a general consensus on the system you should use. Some departments write their own style guides that you will be provided with at the start of your course and expected to follow throughout. Others ask you to learn an established method such as the MLA (Modern Language Association of America), the Harvard, the APA (American Psychological Association), the Chicago or the MHRA (the Modern Humanities Research Association). As is hinted in some of the titles of these organisations, the systems are designed with different disciplines in mind and, as such, prioritise different kinds of information. For example, some highlight the date of original publication of a text while others present only the date of publication of the text that you are using (which may be some centuries after the first printing). Almost more important than knowing which guide to use, however, is the rigid adherence to the one you have chosen. The worst thing you can do is to present an incoherent collage of referencing systems in your essay texts and bibliographies. You can purchase software that formats your references in a particular system and no doubt these will become used more habitually; however, at this stage, it is likely that you will still be responsible for manually formatting your own work at least some of the time. In this chapter we will look in detail at the MLA system (which is representative of the parenthetical style also used by the APA). (The Harvard is representative of the Author–Date system, while the Chicago and MHRA are known as 'note-based' systems.) But first let us remind ourselves of the importance of accurate referencing.

> **Response**
>
> Let's recap: having read this book, what do you feel are the reasons for incorporating extracts and evidence from literary and critical texts in your essays? Why do you need to provide references for these texts?

We are thinking about referencing in the study of literature in particular. Throughout this book we have considered that reading texts and writing about texts are ongoing processes like conversations. We have seen that you can't have a conversation or an argument on your own, and thus your interlocutors must be identified. This is the first and main reason for citing references: to identify your sources, acknowledge the writers you are engaging with. You need to do this in a manner that makes it easy for your reader to locate these texts should she or he so wish, which is the next reason for citing references according to a recognised style. Finally, two more pragmatic reasons for presenting your work according to agreed principles: (1) you'll probably lose marks if you don't, and (2) an original and accurately presented bibliography is some indication that your work is your own and is not plagiarised.

In the following synopsis of the MLA referencing system, I will focus on the two main aspects of referencing in essays and literary assignments: incorporating quotations and sources within the body of your prose (citation), and the bibliography or list of works cited (references). A key difference between the types of referencing system is in the ways that they connect these two sources of information.

6.1 The MLA system

This is a system that was designed specifically for writing about languages and literature. It has another advantage for you too, which is that the rules are contained within an, albeit rather large, reference book (possessed by most academic libraries). As this book runs to 360 pages, you will probably find that you will need to consult the full edition in your library since I am only going to give an overview of the general principles with some basic examples here, but I'd also encourage you to read it for other helpful advice on scholarship at some point: there is a long discussion of plagiarism (as mentioned in chapter 2: Reading); information on research, how to take notes, evaluate them and write summaries; a detailed chapter on the mechanics of writing; information on how to format a paper; and how to write abbreviations as well as how to prepare bibliographies, etc. You could also refer to online sources such as *OWL* (http://owl.english.purdue.edu) for information about the MLA (and the APA) system. I stated above that it is a method characterised by parenthesis: information in brackets in the body of your essay relates to full publication details in your bibliography. (It is the system that I have used in this book.) It is a crucial rule of the MLA system to place the smallest amount of information possible that will make your source clear in the brackets; the system is designed to facilitate *readability* above all, to avoid interrupting the reader's flow.

6.2 Citations in the MLA style

6.2.1 Titles referred to in the body of the essay

Titles of whole texts, including whole journals, films and long poems, everything that has been published in its own right as an independent item, should be <u>underlined</u> or put *in italics*. Every time you mention a text with a short title you should use the title in full, but if you are discussing something with a long title then you must include the full version when you first mention it and subsequently abbreviate it to a recognisable form. (The MLA has its own short titles for individual works of Shakespeare, Chaucer, the books of the Bible and some other canonical literary texts.) Poems, articles and chapters of books should be placed within inverted commas (single if you're in the UK, double in the US) and not underlined or italicised. Here are a few examples:

- *Pride and Prejudice* → no need to abbreviate.
- *The Waste Land* → no need to abbreviate.
- 'The Love Song of J. Alfred Prufrock' → this could be recognisably abbreviated to 'Prufrock' in subsequent citations; abbreviating it to 'Love Song' would be a bit vague.
- *Pan's Labyrinth* → no need to abbreviate.
- *Blast* →no need to abbreviate.
- 'Visual Pleasure and Narrative Cinema' → this could be recognisably abbreviated to 'Visual Pleasure' in subsequent citations.

6.2.2 References in your text

There are several ways of citing sources in your essays. Which of the following do you prefer? (You may wish to refer back to the consideration of passive sentence structures in the last chapter when thinking about this.)

- Fiedler contends that *Slaughterhouse Five* is 'less about Dresden than about [. . .] failure to come to terms with it' (11).
- It has been argued that *Slaughterhouse Five* is 'less about Dresden than about [. . .] failure to come to terms with it' (Fiedler 11).
- It has been argued that *Slaughterhouse Five* is about the inability of society to accept what happened to Dresden (Fiedler 11).

Each version of this sentence is accurately referenced, but most readers find the first version the clearest; it is certainly the most concise. The reference in brackets refers to the full citation of Leslie A. Fiedler's *Kurt Vonnegut: Images and Representations* that is listed in the student's bibliography. In the essay from which this sentence was extracted, only one work by Fiedler was referenced, so this is a simple example. If the author continued to refer to this book by Fiedler, it would only be necessary to include the page number in subsequent brackets. If the page number was the same as the reference immediately before it, '*ibid.*' (abbreviation meaning 'in the same place' in Latin) would be used. There are several more complex cases, however. Here are some examples.

6.2.3 Two or more works by the same author

If you make reference to several works by the same author, but haven't included the name or title in the body of your sentence, you will need to distinguish them by using abbreviated versions of their titles in brackets, for example: (Žižek, *Sublime Object* 37). If you've stated the author's name in the sentence then you only need to give the title and page number in parenthesis: (*Sublime Object* 37); and if you've included both name and title, then only the page reference is required in brackets: (37).

6.2.4 Two or more authors discussed together

In the interests of readability, the MLA discourages long lists of references in parenthesis; however, it's fine to incorporate two or three, in which case you should list them as above with a semi-colon to separate each one: (Sage 23; Snaith 57).

6.2.5 A single work with more than one author or editor

If a work has up to three authors or editors include them all (Gilbert and Gubar 58–62), but if there are more than three you can choose to list them all, or only the first, with the abbreviation '*et al.*', meaning 'and others' in Latin: (Lauter *et al.* 43).

6.2.6 A multi-volume work

Again, if you haven't included the author's name in your text then your parenthesis should look like this: (Woolf 4: 93). If you have, then you simply give the volume number and page number separated by a colon (4: 93).

6.2.7 An introduction, foreword, preface, afterword

Some examples:

- In her introduction to *Voyage in the Dark*, Carole Angier urges the reader to attend to '"looks" and "feelings", not to the words, which belong to the powerful' (Rhys ix).
- Carole Angier urges the reader to attend to '"looks" and "feelings", not to the words, which belong to the powerful' (Rhys, Introd. ix).

You could also write this, if your essay didn't cite the main text of *Voyage in the Dark* by Jean Rhys:

- The introduction to *Voyage in the Dark* urges the reader to attend to '"looks" and "feelings", not to the words, which belong to the powerful' (Angier ix).

6.2.8 A play

If you are writing about a modern or a prose play that is not lineated then refer to the page number: (*The Weir* 37). For other plays, present all the information that is given in the edition; this might be act, scene and line divisions (*Much Ado about Nothing* 2.3.132–8), act and scene (*Lady Windermere's Fan* 1.2) or only lines (*Oedipus Rex* 1435).

6.2.9 Poetry

Again, this rather depends on the amount of information your text provides and also on the length of the poem itself. If it is very short, only a few lines, it is possible to omit a bracketed reference altogether. If it is longer, printed with line numbers, and you have cited the title in your prose then the brackets should contain these numbers and the word 'line/s' so that your reader does not confuse this for a page number: (lines 50–63). If the poem has divisions (books, cantos, stanzas) include these too. Here are some examples:

- Yeats compares the past to a kind of spoilt childhood ('Nineteen Hundred and Nineteen' I.9). 'I' here indicates 'Section I'.
- It is clear that Ovid's *Metamorphoses* is a significant influence on Marvel's 'The Nymph Complaining for the Death of her Fawn' (lines 99–100, 110, 116).
- Extracts of *The Waste Land* have been performed as monologues in their own right ('The Game of Chess' lines 139–72).

6.2.10 An online source

There is a great deal of confusion about the citation and bibliographic record-ing of online and electronic resources, largely because, as the MLA manual identifies, the newness of such media means that standardised rules have not yet been established or agreed upon. Furthermore, because the sources them-selves are not always stable and lasting, there is a need to provide more infor-mation about electronic than print sources.

When referring to a website in the body of your text, you obviously can't list page numbers but you should cite the author, web-page author or, if no author is evident, the title of the page:

- It has been argued that the 'genre-defying' nature of Ballard's novels has led to misleading cover design (Rick McGrath).
- The *Ballardian* is a valuable resource for readers and critics of J. G. Ballard's novels.
- When Salman Rushdie was knighted, sales of *The Satanic Verses* soared (Guardian).

> **Note** If you are discussing a whole text in general, rather than referring to a particular point or including a quotation, there's no need to provide a parenthetical reference. So, for example, in the statement, 'This was the intention of I. A. Richards when he developed his methodology of practical criticism', if there is only one book by Richards in the bibliography no further information is needed in the citation. References should only be supplied when absolutely necessary: remember the principle of readability at all times.

6.2.11 A work with no named author

There are several categories of texts that should be cited according to their title rather than the name of an author or editor. These include periodicals, news-papers, reference works such as dictionaries and encyclopedias, online and electronic resources, official reports and publications, books from the Bible, and, of course, those that are anonymous (which shouldn't be listed under 'Anon.'). You can abbreviate long titles so long as they can still be easily linked to the full publication details in your bibliography.

6.2.12 An indirect source

You should always aim to use the original source but sometimes this isn't pos-sible, for example in the case of recorded speech. Then you put the abbrevi-ation 'qtd. in' before the source that you have used, for example:

- To those who claim that criticism destroys the pleasure of reading Eco offers the rebuttal 'even gynaecologists can fall in love' (qtd. in Currie 25).

6.3 Quotations

Let us remind ourselves of some key points before we consider the presentation of quotations:

- You *do* need to cite literary and critical texts in your essays but these *don't* always have to be as quotations.
- Long extracts and quotations that are not clearly relevant will not enhance your essay and will probably even damage it.
- Think very carefully about the necessity of a quotation before you insert it. Could the information be succinctly summarised? Are you discussing the actual wording of a passage, in which case it should be included? Is a long quotation necessary or could you remove some of it?

6.3.1 Embedded quotations

The MLA guide indicates that quotations that are fewer than four lines of prose in your script should be embedded within a sentence. Since the guide stipulates the size of font and other issues of layout, this is a precise measurement. If you are not following the MLA's font guidelines (for example, because paper sizes are different in the US and the UK) you should embed quotations of about thirty words or fewer. In the UK the quotation should be inside single quotation marks; in the US, they should be double. When your quotation is inserted, the result should be a grammatically correct sentence. Consequently, you may make minor alterations to the original quotation in order to ensure grammatical accuracy and ease of comprehension for your reader. Any changes, editorial intervention, should be included in square brackets; for example, if the original quotation says 'he', you may wish to replace this with '[Kurtz]' so that the reader is clear to whom it refers. The only changes permitted are those necessary to make your presentation and grammar coherent and your sense clear. If you have highlighted a word for emphasis, you must place the phrase '[my emphasis]' in square brackets after it.

Any verse quotation of under three lines should be embedded into your text with a forward slash (/) indicating the line break. In the case of verse, you should keep the capitalisation of the original.

> **Note** Once you have established that your quotation is necessary, you must endeavour to ensure its clarity.

6.3.2 Indented quotations

Any verse quotation of over three lines and any prose quotation of more than forty words (between thirty and forty is at your discretion) should be separated from your writing and will not be included in the word count. You should put a colon to introduce it, then leave one line blank and then indent the extract from your main text. The indentation signals that this is a quotation and so quotation marks are not necessary. For verse, follow the original punctuation, stanza forms and line endings. You should attempt to keep the original appearance of the poem as far as possible – this could be very difficult with some modern verse. Do not use the 'centre text' function on your word-processor as this will be highly distorting. If you are beginning your verse quotation in the middle of a line, try and position the words accordingly, rather than shift them to the left margin. If you are quoting dramatic dialogue or more than one paragraph of prose, you should similarly emulate the original presentation as far as possible.

6.4 Bibliographies and Works Cited in the MLA style

The list of works cited appears at the end of your essay or assignment. This is the list of all the texts that you have referred to in the body of your essay, ordered alphabetically. A bibliography is a more general list of texts that relate to your subject but might not have been expressly mentioned, although you may find the two terms used synonymously. The list should begin on a new but numbered page and it should be titled. Each new entry starts on a new line and if it exceeds one line, the following one/s should be indented. The basic format for an individual entry is:

> Author's name. *Title of book*. Publication place: Publisher, date.
> Freudenberger, Nell. *The Dissident*. New York: Harper Collins, 2006.

You will find details of publication included on one of the first pages before the beginning of the text. Be careful not to confuse the publisher with the printer: printing details are not required. The author's name should be reversed for ease of alphabetisation and recorded as it is given on the book's title page, so, for example, 'Eliot, T. S.' and not 'Eliot, Thomas Stearns'. If an author has a title, Sir or Lady, this should not be included, so 'Lady Mary Wortley Montagu' becomes 'Montagu, Mary Wortley'. I'll now proceed to consider examples of texts with more complicated details.

This is the sequence of information that you might be expected to provide (although not every component will be required for every item):

1 Author
2 Title of item
3 Title of the book
4 Editor, translator, compiler
5 Edition
6 Volume
7 Series title
8 Publication details as follows, Place: Publisher, date.
9 Page numbers

6.4.1 An anthology or compilation

> Rainey, Lawrence, ed. *Modernism: An Anthology.* Oxford: Blackwell Publishing, 2005.

If Rainey was a compiler rather than an editor then the abbreviation would be 'comp.'. If he had several roles then these would all be listed in the order that they appear on the title page.

  If there was more than one editor, this would become 'eds'.

6.4.2 A book by two or more authors

> Leech, Geoffrey N. and Michael H. Short. *Style in Fiction: A Linguistic Introduction to English Fictional Prose.* English Language Series. London and New York: Longman, 1981.

Again, the authors are listed in the order that they appear on the title page; only the first one is reversed. If there are more than three, you can choose either to list them or to give the first one followed by '*et al*.'. If they were editors, compilers or translators, for example, then the appropriate abbreviation should also be given after the final name. Notice that in the example I have given, the book is part of a series and this information is given after the title.

6.4.3 A work in an anthology or a collection of essays

> Stein, Gertrude. *Tender Buttons.* 1914. *Modernism: An Anthology.* Ed. Lawrence Rainey. Oxford: Blackwell Publishing, 2005. 373–99.

You can see from this example that the information about the anthology is needed in addition to the piece you are referring to. Note how the editor of the anthology has moved position and also how I have given the date of the original publication of *Tender Buttons* as well as the book it is anthologised in. Here's another example:

> Marvell, Andrew. 'The Nymph Complaining for the Death of her Fawn'. 1681. *The Poems of Andrew Marvell*. Ed. Nigel Smith. Rev. ed. Harlow: Pearson Education, 2007. 65–71.

The page numbers refer to the whole piece not just to the location of your citation or the quotation you have included.

Here is an example of an essay or chapter in a critical text:

> Steele, Jeffrey. 'The Politics of Mourning: Cultural Grief-Work from Frederick Douglass to Fanny Fern.' *Criticism and the Color Line: Desegregating American Literary Studies*. Ed. Henry B. Wonham. New Brunswick, NJ: Rutgers University Press, 1996. 95–111.

6.4.4 An introduction, preface, foreword or afterword

> Angier, Carole. Introduction. *Voyage in the Dark*. By Jean Rhys. London: Penguin, 2000. v–xiv.

If the introduction, preface or other editorial material was by the same author as the rest of the text, then you need only to write 'By [surname]' after the title. If the introduction itself has a title, this should be inserted in inverted commas before 'Introduction'.

6.4.5 An anonymous book

Don't use 'Anonymous' or 'Anon.', simply start the entry with the title, ignoring 'A', 'An' or 'The'. *New Shorter Oxford English Dictionary*. Oxford: Clarendon Press, 1993.

6.4.6 An edition

> Woolf, Virginia. *Mrs Dalloway*. 1925. Edited and with Introduction and Notes by David Bradshaw. Oxford: Oxford University Press, 2000.

It is not absolutely necessary to include the original date of publication, but I encourage it because I think it is instructive to be aware of the epoch in which a text was first received.

6.4.7 A translation

> Perec, Georges. *Life: A User's Manual.* Trans. David Bellos. London: Vintage, 2003.

If there was an editor too, list the names as they appear on the title page with the appropriate abbreviations.

6.4.8 A book published in a second or subsequent edition

> Chopin, Kate. *The Awakening.* 1899. Ed. Margo Culley. A Norton Critical Edition. 2nd ed. New York: W. W. Norton & Company, 1994.

If it is a revised rather than numbered edition, then insert 'Rev. ed.' after the title or editor as in the Marvell entry above (6.4.3).

6.4.9 A multi-volume work

If you are using more than one volume of a multi-volume work, cite the total number of volumes after the title. Details of page numbers and volume belong in parenthesis in your text.

> Freud, Sigmund. *The Penguin Freud Library.* Trans. James Strachey. 15 vols. Harmondsworth: Penguin, 1974–86.

Notice how the volumes were published over a number of years and this range is included. If the series was not yet complete you would write '4 vols, to date' and include a dash followed by a space after the date '1989– '.

6.4.10 An article in a periodical

> Rowland, Antony. 'Love and Masculinity in the Poetry of Carol Ann Duffy.' *English: The Journal of the English Association* 198 (Autumn 2001): 199–218.

Like a book citation, the information is contained in three parts: author, title and publication details. Some journals have a volume number as well as an issue number; in such cases include this information after the title, as for example, 50.4, followed by the date in brackets. Some don't have a season but just a year, in which case include only this information.

6.4.11 A review

The reviewer's name should be given first, followed by the title of the review (if there is one), then 'Rev. of' followed by the title of the work reviewed, comma, 'by [name of author of work reviewed]', then publication details. Here is an example:

> Thompson, Theresa. Rev. of *Mappings: Feminism and the Cultural Geographies of Encounter*, by Susan Stanford Friedman. *Woolf Studies Annual* 6 (2000): 213–16.

If the review is anonymous, begin with its title or the title of the reviewed work. If it is a review of a performance then also include details of the production after its title.

6.4.12 A film

Unlike books, film references start with the title rather than the author of the screenplay or the director (presumably because this information is often less well known than the title). You must include the director's name, the distributor and year of release but it is up to you whether or not to include other information such as that of the producer and performers. If you are going to include the writer of the screenplay, his or her name comes before the director's.

> *Badlands*. Screenplay and dir. Terrence Malick. Perf. Martin Sheen and Sissy Spacek. Badlands Company, 1973.
>
> *Pan's Labyrinth* [*El Laberinto del Fauno*]. Dir. Guillermo del Toro. Warner Bros Pictures, 2006.

6.4.13 A performance

Entries for performances are similar to those for films: they start with the title, they must include the name of the director and the site at which the performance took place, but you can be selective about whether to include other information or not.

> *The Rose Tattoo*. By Tennessee Williams. Dir. Stephen Pimlott and Nicholas Hytner. Perf. Zoë Wanamaker. National Theatre, London. 29 Jun. 2007.

6.4.14 A letter

A published letter should be treated like a work in a collection (see 6.4.3) but the number of the letter should be added if an editor has given one. (Here the page numbers refer to the individual letter.)

> Huxley, Ernest. 'To Virginia Woolf.' June 1939. Letter 72 of 'The *Three Guineas Letters*.' Ed. Anna Snaith. *Woolf Studies Annual* 6 (2000). 114–34.

A letter that you have received yourself should be listed thus:

> Walker, Alice. Letter to the author. 22 Apr. 2005.
> White, Edmund. Email to the author. 29 Aug. 2004.

6.4.15 An electronic publication

As far as possible you should try and follow the basic principles for book entries and so include the author's name, the title of the document and publication information. The MLA encourages you to record the URL (the web address) in your publication information but warns against misrecording due to the complexity of such addresses. If you are referring to an article on a database with a search engine, it is only necessary to include the URL of the site's search page at the end of that entry. Often it is hard to locate all the information required and, in such instances, you should simply cite whatever you can. Because websites and their addresses are subject to constant change, you must also note the date of access. Here are some examples:

An online book

> Poe, Edgar Allan. *A Descent into the Maelstrom. The Literature Network.* 23 Feb. 2007 http://www.online-literature.com/poe/26/.

If an editor or translator had been given this information would have appeared after the title of the text and before the name of the site.

An entire site

> *Project Gutenberg.* 13 Apr. 2006. http://promo.net/pg/.

Again, if an editor had been listed this would have been included after the title.

An article in a newspaper

> Meeks, James. 'Look back in anger.' *Guardian Unlimited.* 27 Jun. 2007 http://books.guardian.co.uk/interviews/story/0,,2109580,00.html.

Works cited

American Psychological Association. *Publication Manual of the American Psychological Association.* 5th ed. Washington, DC: APA, 2001.

The Chicago Manual of Style. 15th ed. Chicago and London: University of Chicago Press, 2003.

Cook, Malcolm *et al. MHRA Style Guide: A Handbook for Authors, Editors, and Writers of Theses.* London: Modern Humanities Research Association, 2002.

Gibaldi, Joseph. *MLA Handbook for Writers of Research Papers.* 6th ed. New York: The Modern Language Association of America, 2003.

OWL. The Online Writing Lab at Purdue. http://owl.english.purdue.edu

Sample essay by Alex Hobbs

Here is an essay that was written by a student in her first year of study for a degree in English and American Literature at the Open University. It has been reproduced in its entirety and its original format without any editorial alteration or correction. You can read it independently in order to examine the features of a strong essay but you'll also find more detailed methods of analysing it on pages 82, 109 and 113 in chapter 4: Essays. You could also reformat it in the MLA style for textual references if you want to practise referencing methods.

"The model of individual triumph over adversity tends to undermine the pleas for social reform at the heart of all antebellum slave narratives." (David Van Leer, 128, Sundquist) Do you agree?

Slave narratives had a gripping story line, which captured the reader in the same way as picaresque and sentimental novels. Due to this, they were bestsellers; as Baker notes, they were widely translated and cheaply available, and as a result "sold by the thousands"[1]. However, these were autobiographies and so contained truth, this strengthened the impact of the story for the reader. Whether the slave directly called for social reform in their narrative or whether it can be inferred, it is certain that by writing this literature, the author hoped to influence attitudes concerning black people in American society.

It could be argued that these narratives are so full of personal detail because they are cathartic, as Lee notes these stories were written as "an act of memorialization."[2] Moreover, to tell this story was in itself an assertion of freedom. By writing personal experiences, several objectives could be accomplished: firstly, a traumatic experience was exorcised; secondly, the story would reach more people than by word of mouth;

---

[1]   Houston A. Baker Jr, Narrative of the Life of Frederick Douglass, an American Slave (Introduction), pp.9

[2]   A. Robert Lee, Designs of Blackness: Mappings in the Literature and Culture of Afro-America, pp.26

and thirdly, the black author could prove to racist whites that they were capable of artistic and intellectual thoughts. Personal achievement was an important issue to the slave, or ex-slave, as in slavery their individuality was not respected, nor indeed was it permitted. Thus, the slave worked to put his or her personal mark upon the text, even in obvious ways; as Gates notices in Equiano's narrative: "the subtle, "Written by Himself" and a signed engraving of the black author"[3]. Gates argues that this shows the author asserting ownership over his own work; an interpreted extension of this is that the ex-slave was also claiming autonomy over himself, over his body and mind.

Certainly, catharsis was not all the authors hoped to achieve otherwise it would not have been necessary to publish. However, these texts were published, and although personal protest was one reason for this, to influence the opinions of others was another. As Bontemps asserts of Douglass' work, and it is true of countless others: "He had not written for his own amusement. He was still fighting slavery."[4] Many of the writers, including Douglass, Equiano and Jacobs, were involved with the northern abolitionists; it was these men and women who authenticated their work in covering letters. The abolitionists had some influence upon the narratives, not in the actual writing, but in what was written and how. Steele maintains that white abolitionists sought to keep slave narratives personal rather than political, so as not to affront the average white reader. Wendell Phillips, who wrote an introductory letter for Douglass, believed that any direct criticism of slavery would weaken the impact of the slave's traumatic story. It seems that the abolitionists knew, like the feminists of over a hundred years later, that a personal story could have a political effect, if were written to suit the audience. Thus, many of the narratives were written with a strong sentimental and elegiac tone to induce sympathy, especially in female readers. By eloquently describing their personal experiences in slavery, the reader is left with two overriding feelings: the horror of that individual's experience and, as Lauret notes: "the absurdity of that condition for one so eloquent, so cultured, and so rational as the text revealed its author to be."[5]

Equiano's narrative, became a model that many other ex-slaves would follow. However, this was not because his experience in slavery was common, it was not, rather it was the style in which it was written and

---

[3] Henry Louis Gates, Jr., The Signifying Monkey, pp.153

[4] Arna Bontemps, Free At Last: The Life of Frederick Douglass, pp.99

[5] Maria Lauret, Beginning Ethnic American Literatures, pp.67

the structure of the work that was imitated. Equiano begins by recalling his homeland, modern day Nigeria, with happiness; he gives the reader a very colourful description, drawing them in with exotic details of everyday life and customs in his village. Owing to his removed status, he can act as an anthropologist, informing the reader of the religion, population, and buildings; for example: "We are almost a nation of dancers, musicians, and poets. Thus every great event, such as a triumphant return from battle or other cause of public rejoicing, is celebrated in public dances, which are accompanied with songs and music suited to the occasion."[6] The effect is a simple, but enchanting vision; Equiano never gives the reader the impression of uncivilised or heathen ways. Even though he later undergoes a conversion to Christianity, he maintains his fondness for his home and people. Due to this safe image of home, Equiano's capture seems all the more brutal to the reader.

Although Equiano does not seem to be particularly badly treated in the physical sense, perhaps because he did not experience plantation life, there is a notion of mental containment and torture. Equiano is repeatedly parted from his family, something that causes him great anguish. He is also left in confusion over his identity:

> "In this place I was called Jacob; but on board the *African Snow*, I was called Michael. . . . While I was on board this ship, my captain and master named me *Gustavus Vassa*. . . [I] refused to be called so, and told him as well as I could that I would be called Jacob; but he said I should not, and still called me Gustavus: and when I refused to answer to my new name, which I at first did, it gained me many a cuff; so at length I submitted, and by which I have been known ever since."[7]

This not only shows his confusion, but also the arrogance of the white master; Pascal believes he has the right to enforce an identity upon another through violence.

Perhaps Equiano wrote too early to make too much of a comment upon the social reform that writers such as Douglass were campaigning for more than fifty years later. However, he does strive to buy his freedom, which he finally does, he also entreats his reader to treat slaves, or indeed ex-slaves, as equals. This is powerful in the text as he addresses

---

6   Olaudah Equiano, *The Interesting Narrative of the Life of Olaudah Equiano, or Gustavus Vassa, the African. Written By Himself (The Heath Anthology Vol.I)*, pp.1120

7   Olaudah Equiano, *The Interesting Narrative of the Life of Olaudah Equiano, or Gustavus Vassa, the African. Written By Himself (The Heath Anthology Vol.I)*, pp.1136-7

the reader directly: "O, ye nominal Christians! might not an African ask you – Learned you this from your God, who says unto you, Do unto all men as you would men should do unto you?"[8] Thus, Equiano simultaneously highlights the religious impropriety and immorality of slavery and furthermore, questions the values of those involved with it.

Jacobs also begins her tale happily, she writes that she did not realise she was a slave until her mother's death: "I never dreamed I was a piece of merchandise. . .liable to be demanded of them at any moment."[9] Her humiliation is furthered as she is bequeathed to a five-year-old girl. She feels indignation at this because her previous mistress had been so kind to her, teaching her basic literacy and the bible, and she comments upon the irony of this:

> "My mistress had taught me the precepts of God's Word: "Thou shalt love they neighbor as thyself." "Whatsoever ye would that men should do unto you, do ye even so to them." But I was her slave, and I suppose she did not recognize me as her neighbor."[10]

This has much the same effect upon the reader as Equiano's use of religion had, condemning the white southerners for their contradictory Christian values.

The fact that Jacobs, or Linda Brent as she calls herself, is a woman seems to add impact to her narrative. Jacob's account is extremely personal, as it deals with the violation of her person, not simply her containment, as was true of all slaves, Dr. Flint's desires to command her sexually. Although Brent does managed to win some small victories through her own wit, such as feigning illiteracy so she cannot read his coarse notes, the situation builds up until it is unbearable and even life threatening. Moreover, her mistress will not help her; Jacob's depicts white woman completely devoid of pity:

> "She felt her marriage were desecrated, her dignity insulted; but she had no compassion for the poor victim of her husband's perfidy. She pitied herself as a martyr; but she was incapable of feeling for the condition of shame and misery in which her unfortunate, helpless slave was placed."[11]

[8] Olaudah Equiano, The Interesting Narrative of the Life of Olaudah Equiano, or Gustavus Vassa, the African. Written By Himself (The Heath Anthology Vol.I), pp.1135
[9] Harriet Jacobs, Incidents in the Life of a Slave Girl (Heath anthology Vol.1), pp.1962
[10] Harriet Jacobs, Incidents in the Life of a Slave Girl (Heath anthology Vol.1), pp.1964
[11] Harriet Jacobs, Incidents in the Life of a Slave Girl (Heath anthology Vol.1), pp.1966

Thus, her only escape is to sleep with another white man and become pregnant so her master will not want her. Whilst Brent is working on the plantation, leaving her children with her grandmother each day, she hears that her children will also be put to work. She cannot bear this, and so puts herself in danger by taking the children and running away. Though she has to stay in hiding for years, she finally triumphs and reaches the north, however, even here she was not safe from the clutches of her former slaveholders due to the Fugitive Slave Law. This threat of recapture keeps her from her grandmother, something which she feels keenly: "her messages of love made my heart yearn to see her before she died, and I mourned over the fact that it was impossible."[12] Therefore, although there is triumph in her escape, she is still tortured by separation.

Certainly, Jacobs' work is highly personal dealing, as it does, with her own story, yet she published under a pseudonym. The story is a traumatic one, and that she distances herself from it is understandable. As Yellin comprehends, using her own name would have meant "to expose her own sexual history and reveal herself as an unwed mother."[13] She continues to comment that the narrative loses none of its poignancy, as it is still a first-person account. Her story is doubtlessly effectual in itself but, like Equiano, the moments when she addresses her reader directly give this text more impact. For example, she justifies her actions in sleeping with another white man as necessary, and implores the reader not to judge her as they would a white woman: "Pity me, and pardon me, O virtuous reader! You never knew what it is to be a slave; to be entirely unprotected by law or custom; to have the laws reduce you to the position of a chattel, entirely subject to the will of another."[14] Thus, if the reader had not felt sympathy before, simply from the account, she is coerced into sympathy now, as otherwise it seems she has no sense of compassion, like Mrs. Flint. It is clear that the characters of Mrs. Flint and Mrs. Dodge are meant to be didactic; their names themselves indicate their personalities, one will show her slave no kindness, the other is willing to help the woman out of slavery using her own money.

It should be noted that Jacobs does not only tell her own story but also that of Aunt Nancy; resulting from her duties, this woman can never bring her pregnancies to term, all her children die prematurely and

---

[12] Harriet Jacobs, Incidents in the Life of a Slave Girl (Heath anthology Vol.1), pp.1981
[13] Jean Fagan Yellin, The Heath Anthology of American Literature Vol.1, pp.1961
[14] Harriet Jacobs, Incidents in the Life of a Slave Girl (Heath anthology Vol.1), pp.1970

finally she also dies. Steele argues that it is through the inclusion of this story that Jacobs shows the extent to which slavery affects women: "this chapter. . .quickly becomes a lament for all black women injured by the institution of slavery. In this regard, Nancy's failure to become a mother seems symbolic of one of the harshest aspects of slavery – its threat to maternity and the mother–child bond."[15] Thus, although her own personal account ends with triumph, Jacobs clarifies that many black women do not achieve this. This leaves the restoration of moral order hanging; she is leaving some of the burden of rectifying this to her white female readers.

Douglass' story also includes personal detail; his account begins with his personal history, as much as he knows it. He begins by saying he has no knowledge of his age, this at once shows how slavery can strip a man of his identity, a birthday is universal but Douglass is denied one. His identity is further limited because he was taken away from his mother at a young age. He comments that this experience was not isolated:

> "It is a common custom, in the part of Maryland from which I ran away, to part children from their mothers at a very early age . . . . For what this separation is done, I do not know, unless it be to hinder the development of the child's affection toward its mother, and to blunt and destroy the natural affection of the mother for the child. This is the inevitable result."[16]

He is also denied a father, he writes: "My father was a white man. He was admitted to be by all I ever heard speak of my parentage. The opinion was also whispered that my master was my father; but of the correctness of this opinion, I know nothing; the means of knowing was withheld from me."[17] Despite this being his personal history, this history was shared by innumerable plantation slaves. Consequently, Douglass shows that in slavery a man has no other identity than that of his position as a slave. Lee comments that by asserting his father as a white man, Douglass is also stressing the concept of race within society: "he raises the issue . . . of the whole arbitrariness of 'race' ".[18] Slave owners believed that blacks were inferior and therefore deserved slavery, but Douglass is questioning this, he asserts his white blood to show that they do not recognise any difference between individuals.

[15] Jeffrey Steele, Criticism and the Color Line, pp.102
[16] Frederick Douglass, Narrative of the Life of Frederick Douglass, an American Slave, pp.48
[17] Frederick Douglass, Narrative of the Life of Frederick Douglass, an American Slave, pp.48
[18] A. Robert Lee, *Designs of Blackness: Mappings in the Literature and Culture of Afro-America*, pp.28

Apart from his escape to the north, which is clearly triumphant, the most symbolic victory is his fight with Covey. The fight builds up over a period of a few days. It begins with an initial burst of violence on the overseer's part whilst Douglass is sick in the fields, he then goes to complain to his master, but he takes Covey's side saying Douglass must have done something to prompt such a punishment. Thus, Douglass must return and face Covey; Covey captures him alone in the stable and sets about whipping him, it is at this point that Douglass decides to assert himself, and fights back. Douglass punishes Covey for his treatment of him as a slave: "He asked me if I meant to persist in my resistance. I told him I did, come what might; that he had used me like a brute for six months, and that I was determined to be used so no longer."[19] The final victory comes after a two hour struggle and Covey concedes; Douglass notes that after this, Covey, though he threatened to, never struck him again. By asserting himself thus, Douglass comments: "You have seen how a man was made a slave; you shall see how a slave was made a man."[20] These images are so powerful, that this event ceases to be a fight between two men, but becomes representative of the entire struggle of slaves over those who enslave them, much as Mohammed Ali fights against white fighters became symbols of the civil rights struggles in the 1960s.

In the appendix, Douglass changes his focus from personal experience; he concentrates instead on religion. He wants to clarify the difference between the so-called Christian practices operating in America under slavery and real Christianity, of which slavery is an abomination. With emotive and repetitive language Douglass impresses upon the reader his disgust that slave holders considered themselves Christian, he writes: "I love the pure, peaceable, and impartial Christianity of Christ: I therefore hate the corrupt, slaveholding, women-whipping, cradle-plundering, partial and hypocritical Christianity of this land."[21] He takes all the facets of Christianity and shows how slavery has corrupted them; for example, Christians exhort the importance of family, while slaveholders divide entire families. Moreover, he does not just blame those directly involved with slavery, he argues that Christians should feel a sense of duty to keep true Christian values prevalent in America. Thus, Douglass is inciting his reader into acting upon the cause of abolition through questioning their moral values.

[19] Frederick Douglass, *Narrative of the Life of Frederick Douglass, an American Slave*, pp.112
[20] Frederick Douglass, *Narrative of the Life of Frederick Douglass, an American Slave*, pp.107
[21] Frederick Douglass, Narrative of the Life of Frederick Douglass, an American Slave, pp.153

Therefore, although it is obvious that the experiences of these three ex-slaves are profoundly different, the effect of their work upon their readers was similar because they employed many of the same literary tactics. The authors addressed issues that would shock the white reader; scenes physical violence and the mental turmoil from separation from their families were particularly effective. Separation especially appealed to the sensibilities of women readers. This was particularly poignant when written by a woman slave as this added a sexual and moral dimension. In Jacobs' narrative Lauret notes: "The subtext, of course, involved another question; how could white women condone the abuse of black women's bodies as labourers and mistresses, breeder of slaves and sexual servants, by their own husbands, their own fathers, their own brothers."[22] Certainly the stories themselves invoked sympathy, but the authors tired to exacerbate this by speaking to the reader directly about the morality of slavery, and as an extension, the morality of the reader for failing to act against this.

It must also be considered that their readership was two-fold, certainly they wrote to convince whites against slavery, but also to inspire black people to join the abolitionist cause. For this reason personal experiences were very important as they would act as motivation; indeed, even in the sixties Douglass remained an honoured figure, for example there is a poster of him in the narrator's office in Ellison's *Invisible Man.*

It is difficult to argue that social reform has been overshadowed by individual accounts when these authors were so instrumental in the fight against slavery, each one of them was politically involved with abolition. Equiano was dedicated to the abolition cause in England, he wrote letters to newspapers, officials and even Queen Charlotte admonishing slavery. Jacobs ran an Anti-Slavery Reading Room in Rochester, concerning herself particularly with the plight of female slaves. Douglass, of course, was very active in abolitionist circles, frequently seen at northern conventions. Thus, these narratives can be seen as a highly effective extension of this work. Through writing the authors were able to reach a wider audience, they were already telling their life stories orally, but were able to go into explicit detail in their narratives. Indeed, these narratives did have the effect that they were intended to; they influenced the opinion of their readers. This is a response of a woman reader to Douglass' narrative but it is certainly applicable to all three: "Never before have I been brought so completely in sympathy with the slave.

[22] Maria Lauret, *Beginning Ethnic American Literatures,* pp.69

May the author become a mighty instrument to the pulling down of the strongholds of iniquity, and the establishment of righteousness in our land."[23] With public opinion changed in the favour of the slave, it would then be possible to seek support for abolition more widely. In other words, by reaching the reader on a personal level the author had also succeeded in altering their political opinions.

In conclusion, these slave narratives do put particular emphasis on personal details, but then their personal achievements were so great considering the adversities they had to contend with. Moreover, by doing so they could reach their reader on a personal level, changing their views about one black person instead of the institution of slavery. But by doing so the reader came to doubt the propriety of such a system for people who were so honourable in their lives. If their life stories could not achieve this then the author also played upon their perceived Christianity, condemning them for acting against religious teachings. Thus, social reform is at the centre of all these narratives, it is simply not as obvious as political rhetoric, but arguably this more emotional form of literature is just as effective.

Works cited in Alex's essay (in the MLA style)

Bontemps, Arna. *Free at Last: The Life of Frederick Douglass.* New York: Dodd, Mead & Company, 1971.

Douglass, Frederick. *Narrative of the Life of Frederick Douglass, an American Slave, Written by Himself.* 1845. Ed. and intro. Houston A. Baker, Jr. New York: Penguin, 1986.

Equiano, Olaudah. *The Interesting Narrative of the Life of Olaudah Equiano, or Gustavus Vassa, the African. Written by Himself.* 1789. *The Heath Anthology of American Literature.* Ed. Paul Lauter *et al.* 4th ed. Vol. 1. Boston: Houghton, 2002. 1118–49.

Gates, Henry Louis, Jr. *The Signifying Monkey: A Theory of Afro-American Literary Criticism.* New York and Oxford: Oxford University Press, 1988.

Jacobs, Harriet Ann. *Incidents in the Life of a Slave Girl.* 1861. *The Heath Anthology of American Literature.* Ed. Paul Lauter *et al.* 4th ed. Vol. 1. Boston: Houghton, 2002. 1962–85.

Lauret, Maria. 'African American Fiction.' *Beginning Ethnic American Literatures.* Ed. Helena Grice *et al.* Manchester: Manchester University Press, 2001. 64–132.

Lee, A. Robert. *Designs of Blackness: Mappings in the Literature and Culture of Afro-America.* London: Pluto Press, 1998.

---

[23]   Arna Bontemp, Free At Last: The Life of Frederick Douglass, pp.100

Steele, Jeffrey. 'The Politics of Mourning: Cultural Grief-Work from Frederick
    Douglass to Fanny Fern.' *Criticism and the Color Line: Desegregating
    American Literary Studies.* Ed. Henry B. Wonham. New Brunswick, NJ:
    Rutgers University Press, 1996. 95–111.
Van Leer, David. 'Reading Slavery: The Anxiety of Ethnicity in Douglass's *Narrative.*'
    Frederick Douglass: New Literary and Historical Essays. Ed. Eric J. Sundquist.
    New York: Cambridge University Press, 1990. 118–40.
Yellin, Jean Fagan, 'Harriet Ann Jacobs 1813–1897.' *The Heath Anthology of American
    Literature.* Ed. Paul Lauter *et al.* 4th ed. Vol. 1. Boston: Houghton, 2002.
    1960 1.

Index

Page numbers in *italic* refer to boxed inserts